MIRACLES
IN AMERICAN HISTORY
32 Amazing Stories of Answered Prayer

———◆———

SUSIE FEDERER
Adapted from William J. Federer's "American Minute"

Miracles in American History -32 Amazing Stories of Answered Prayer
by Susie Federer
(adapted from William J. Federer's American Minute)

For other, contact: Amerisearch, Inc., P.O. Box 20163 St. Louis, MO 63123
314-487-4395, 314-487-4489 fax 1-888-USA-WORD
www.amerisearch.net   wjfederer@gmail.com

HISTORY/RELIGIOUS/EDUCATION
ISBN 978-0-9827101-9-7   paperback
ISBN ebook

Cover design by DustinMyersDesign.com   573-308-6060

Amerisearch, Inc., P.O. Box 20163, St. Louis, MO 63123
1-888-USA-WORD, 314-487-4395, 314-487-4489 fax
www.amerisearch.net, wjfederer@gmail.com

Because America needs a miracle today...

———◆———

"The Hand of Providence has been so conspicuous in all this - the course of the war - that he must be worse than an infidel that lacks faith."

-General George Washington, August 20, 1778

—◦—◦—

DEDICATION

I dedicate this book to my greatest gifts from God, my four amazing children: Jessica Joy, William Gabriel, Katharine Melody and Richard Michael. I love you!

I must acknowledge my brother John and his wife Sharon who took me in when I lost my parents as a teenager and raised me with the love of Jesus. John, you will always be my hero. I love you!

To Don and Katharine Frank who were parents to me in Texas and whom we love so dearly.

And to Foster & Lynn Friess, and Steve & Polly Friess who have been such tremendous friends, helping us to affect the nation. You were there at a key turning point, with the glorious example of your lives and the love of Christ. We love you and your beautiful family!

- Susie Federer, May 14, 2012

"This glorious revolution...distinguished by so many marks of the Divine favor and interposition...in a manner so singular, and I may say miraculous, that when future ages shall read its history they will be tempted to consider a great part of it as fabulous...Will it not appear extraordinary...like the emancipation of the Jews from Egyptian servitude."

-Chief Justice John Jay, September 8, 1777

CONTENTS

INTRODUCTION

My husband William J. Federer has been compiling quotes from great men and women throughout history for over 25 years. He has written 20 books, produced several DVD's, has a television show called *Faith in History* on the TCT network, and a daily radio feature called *American Minute*, which airs on great networks like the Bott Radio Network, the VCY Network, and others.

Bill speaks constantly across America in schools, seminars, universities, churches, military bases, and conferences to reignite a passion in Americans to preserve our Judeo-Christian heritage. I listen to him all the time and get so inspired when he gets to the part of how God moved when Presidents and other great leaders prayed, that I decided to compile this book.

At a time when our country is facing so many crises, it is important for Americans to remember that in past times of national crises we took courage, prayed and saw hopeless situations turn around.

I encourage you to read these stories of faith and miraculous answers to prayer to your children and grandchildren. Share them with friends and coworkers.

Encourage them that God will not only turn their lives around, but will turn this nation around as well. God will protect us and bless us if we repent, seek His face, and strive to do His will for our lives.

Please pray the prayer at the end of this book and add your own prayers. I truly believe God will answer our prayers for this nation miraculously if we all "seek ye first the Kingdom of God." I believe in miracles because I have depended upon them to survive. You will too after you read these true, inspiring stories of Divine intervention!

God bless you and your loved ones, and God bless America!

"America is another name for opportunity.

Our whole history appears like a last effort of Divine
Providence in behalf of the human race."
-Ralph Waldo Emerson

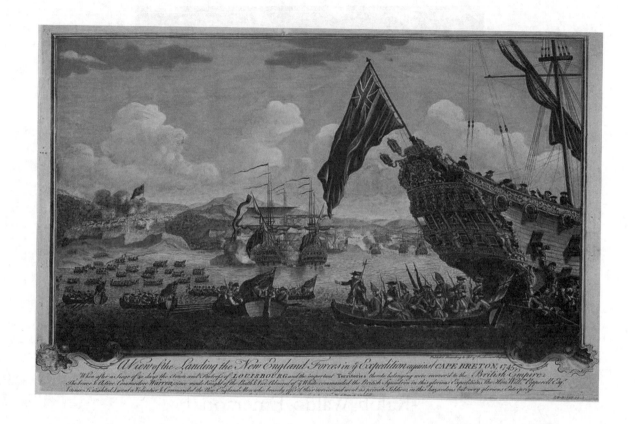

1.
AFTER PRAYER,
HURRICANE SCATTERS ENEMY FLEET

In 1731, a Spanish commander cut off the ear of British Captain Robert Jenkins and told him to take it to his King. This began the War of Jenkins' Ear. British Admiral Edward Vernon, with George Washington's half-brother, Lawrence, sailed to Panama and captured the Spanish city of Porto Bello, but failed to take Cartagena, Columbia. In the Admiral's honor, Washington's farm was named Mount Vernon.

In 1742, after Maria Theresa became the first woman on Austria's throne, the War of Austrian Succession brought Prussia and France into war with England. In America, this was called King George's War. In 1745, the British took the French city of Louisbourg, Nova Scotia, which had been New France's second most important commercial city after Quebec, and third busiest seaport in America, behind Boston and Philadelphia.

France wanted Louisbourg back, and in 1746, King Louis XV sent Admiral d'Anville with the most powerful fleet of its day: 73 ships with 800 cannons and 13,000 troops. Admiral d'Anville intended to "expel the British from Nova Scotia, consign Boston to flames, ravage New England, and waste the British West Indies."

Massachusetts Governor William Shirley declared a Day of Prayer and Fasting, October 16, 1746, to pray for deliverance. Boston citizens gathered in the Old South Meeting House, where Rev. Thomas Prince prayed: "Send Thy tempest, Lord, upon the water...scatter the ships of our tormentors!"

Historian Catherine Drinker Bowen related that as he finished praying, the sky darkened, winds shrieked and church bells rang "a wild, uneven sound...though no man was in the steeple." A hurricane scattered the entire French fleet as far as the Caribbean. Lightning struck several ships, igniting gunpowder magazines, causing explosions and fire.

With 2,000 dead, including Admiral d'Anville, and 4,000 sick with typhoid, French Vice-Admiral d'Estournelle threw himself on his sword.

Henry Wadsworth Longfellow wrote in his poem, *The Ballad of the French Fleet*:

Admiral d'Anville had sworn by cross and crown,
To ravage with fire and steel our helpless Boston Town...
There were rumors in the street, in the houses there was fear
Of the coming of the fleet, and the danger hovering near.
And while from mouth to mouth, spread the tidings of dismay,
I stood in the Old South, saying humbly: "Let us pray!"
"Oh Lord! we would not advise; but if in thy Providence
A tempest should arise, to drive the French Fleet hence,

And scatter it far and wide, or sink it in the sea,
We should be satisfied, and Thine the glory be..."
Like a potter's vessel broke, the great ships of the line...
Were carried away as smoke...or sank in the brine.

As threats continued from France and Spain, a Great Awakening Revival spread throughout the colonies. A printer in Philadelphia named Ben Franklin organized Pennsylvania's first "volunteer" militia and proposed a General Fast, which was approved by Pennsylvania's President and Council, and published in the *Pennsylvania Gazette*, December 12, 1747:

> The calamities of a bloody war...seem every year more nearly to approach us...and there is just reason to fear that unless we humble ourselves before the Lord and amend our ways, we may be chastized with yet heavier judgments.
>
> We have...thought fit...to appoint...a Day of Fasting & Prayer, exhorting all, both Ministers & People...to join with one accord in the most humble & fervent supplications that Almighty God would mercifully interpose and still the rage of war among the nations & put a stop to the effusion of Christian blood.

Their prayers were answered as Philadelphia was not attacked.

2.
WASHINGTON HAD 4 BULLETS THROUGH HIS COAT, YET UNHARMED

Tensions between Britain's King George II and France's King Louis XV exploded into the first global war - the Seven Years War, called in America the French and Indian War. It was sparked by the ambush in 1754 of a French detachment in the Ohio Valley by British militia led by 22-year-old Virginia Colonel George Washington. It spread to every major power in Europe and their colonies in the Caribbean, India, Philippines and Africa. Over a million died.

1,400 British troops marched over the Appalachian Mountains to seize French Fort Duquesne, near present day Pittsburgh. One of the wagon drivers was 21-year-old Daniel Boone. On July 9, 1755, as they passed through a deep wooded ravine along the Monongahela

River eight miles south of the fort, they were ambushed by French regulars, Canadians, and Potawatomi and Ottawa Indians. Not accustomed to fighting unless in an open field, over 900 British soldiers were annihilated in the Battle of the Wilderness, or Battle of Monongahela.

Col. George Washington rode back and forth during the battle delivering orders for General Edward Braddock, the Commander-in-Chief of British forces in America. Eventually, Braddock was killed and every officer on horseback was shot, except Washington. Washington carried Braddock from the field. Braddock's field desk was captured, revealing all the British military plans, enabling the French to surprise and defeat British forces in the battles at Fort Oswego, Fort William Henry, Fort Duquesne, and Carillon. These British losses convinced the Iroquois tribes of Senecas and Cayugas to switch their allegiances to the French.

Before he died Braddock gave Washington his battle uniform sash, which Washington reportedly carried with him the rest of his life, even while Commander-in-Chief and President. Washington presided at the burial service for General Braddock, as the chaplain was wounded. Braddock's body was buried in the middle of the road so as to prevent it from being found and desecrated.

Shortly thereafter, writing from Fort Cumberland, George Washington described the Battle of Monongahela to his younger brother, John Augustine Washington, July 18, 1755:

> As I have heard, since my arrival at this place, a circumstantial account
> of my death and dying speech, I take this early opportunity of contradicting
> the first, and of assuring you, that I have not as yet composed the latter.

But by the All-Powerful Dispensations of Providence, I have been protected beyond all human probability or expectation; for I had four bullets through my coat, and two horses shot under me, yet escaped unhurt, although death was leveling my companions on every side of me!

An Indian warrior later declared:

Washington was never born to be killed by a bullet! I had seventeen fair fires at him with my rifle and after all could not bring him to the ground!

3.
THE BOSTON TEA PARTY, HARBOR BLOCKED & JEFFERSON'S "FASTING" RESOLUTION

The French and Indian War ended in 1763 with the French losing Canada and all their land east of the Mississippi River. King George III decided to tax the colonies to pay for their defense in case of future French incursions or native uprisings. British troops were funded by the Sugar Tax of 1764, Stamp Tax of 1765 and Townshend Acts of 1767, taxing glass, paint and paper. As the Colonies had no representative in Parliament, the cry arose, "No taxation without representation." The King imposed Writs of Assistance in 1765 allowing British authorities to arrest anybody, anytime, anywhere on any suspicion, and to detain them indefinitely. Citizens' houses, property and farms could be taken without a warrant or due process.

As there were no barracks, British troops forcibly lodged or "quartered" in citizens' homes, leaving families to live in barns, basements or attics. On March 5, 1770, a mob formed in Boston to protest, and in the confusion British troops fired into the crowd, killing five, one of which was the African American patriot, Crispus Attucks. This became known as the Boston Massacre.

In 1773, the British passed the Tea Act, in which the King showed favoritism by allowing the East India Tea Company to sell a half million pounds of tea in the Colonies with no taxes, giving them a monopoly by underselling American merchants.

On December 16, 1773, Sam Adams led some citizens of Boston, called Sons of Liberty, to disguise themselves as Mohawk Indians and raid the British ships at Griffin's Wharf, throwing 342 chests of British East India Company tea into Boston's harbor. This became known as the Boston Tea Party.

The King responded with the Boston Port Act, punishing the colonists by blockading Boston's harbor on June 1, 1774. In the neighboring colony of Virginia, Thomas Jefferson drafted a Day of Fasting to be observed the same day. It was introduced into the Virginia House of Burgesses by Robert Carter Nicholas with the support of Patrick Henry, Richard Henry Lee and George Mason, and passed unanimously:

> This House, being deeply impressed with apprehension of the great dangers, to be derived to British America, from the hostile invasion of the City of Boston, in our sister Colony of Massachusetts...deem it highly necessary that the said first day of June be set apart, by the members of this House as a Day of Fasting, Humiliation and Prayer,

devoutly to implore the Divine interposition, for averting the heavy calamity which threatens destruction to our civil rights...

Ordered, therefore that the Members of this House do attend...with the Speaker, and the mace, to the Church in this City, for the purposes aforesaid; and that the Reverend Mr. Price be appointed to read prayers, and the Reverend Mr. Gwatkin, to preach a sermon.

George Washington wrote in his diary, June 1, 1774:

"Went to church, fasted all day."

Virginia's Royal Governor, Lord Dunmore viewed the Fasting Resolution as a veiled protest against King George III, as it was the King's policy which was responsible for blockading Boston's Harbor. Lord Dunmore dissolved the House of Burgesses.

Rather than going home, the Virginia Legislators gathered down the street at Raleigh Tavern, where in the back room they conspired to form the first Continental Congress, which met three months later in Philadelphia.

Within two years, the Continental Congress voted for independence.

4.
BATTLE OF LEXINGTON & CONCORD

September 7, 1774, the Continental Congress met in Philadelphia. John Adams wrote:

When Congress met, Mr. Cushing made a motion that it should be opened with Prayer. It was opposed by Mr. Jay of New York and Mr. Rutledge of South Carolina because we were so divided in religious sentiments, some Episcopalians, some Quakers, some Anabaptists, some Presbyterians, and some Congregationalists...Mr. Samuel Adams arose and said that he was no bigot, and could hear a Prayer from any gentleman of Piety and virtue, who was at the same time a friend to his Country...

Next morning Rev. Mr. Duche'...read several prayers... and...the 35th Psalm... I never saw a greater effect upon an audience. It seemed as if heaven had ordained that Psalm to be read on that morning. After this, Mr. Duche', unexpectedly to everybody, struck out into an extemporary prayer, which filled the bosom of every man present. I must confess, I never heard a better prayer.

Six months after the Continental Congress first met was the Battle of Lexington and Concord. On April 15, 1775, the Massachusetts Provincial Congress, led by John Hancock, declared:

> In circumstances dark as these, it becomes us, as men and Christians, to reflect that, whilst every prudent measure should be taken to ward off the impending judgments...the 11th of May next be set apart as a Day of Public Humiliation, Fasting and Prayer...to confess their sins...to implore the Forgiveness of all our Transgression.

The British planned a preemptive strike by marching to Lexington and Concord to seize their guns and arrest Samuel Adams, John Hancock, and other Revolutionary leaders. Henry Wadsworth Longfellow's poem, *Paul Revere's Ride*, described how patriots sent a warning from Boston's Old North Church to the people of Lexington and Concord that the British were coming:

> Listen my children and you shall hear
> of the midnight ride of Paul Revere...
> Hang a lantern aloft in the belfry arch...
> One if by land, two if by sea...

Though Paul Revere was captured, William Dawes and Samuel Prescott continued their ride. In early dawn, April 19, 1775, American "Minutemen," as poet Ralph Waldo Emerson wrote, fired the "shot heard round the world" by confronting the British on Lexington Green and at Concord's Old North Bridge.

The same day, April 19, 1775, Connecticut Governor Jonathan Trumbull proclaimed a Day of Fasting, that:

> God would graciously pour out His Holy Spirit on us to bring us to a thorough repentance and effectual reformation that our iniquities may not be our ruin; that He would restore, preserve and secure the liberties of this and all the other British American colonies, and make the land a mountain of Holiness, and habitation of righteousness forever.

New England celebrates April 19th as "Patriots' Day."

Ralph Waldo Emerson wrote *The Concord Hymn* in 1837 to dedicate the monument where the battle of Concord's North Bridge took place, April 19, 1775. At the base of Daniel Chester French's "Minute Man Statue," are lines from the poem's most famous stanza:

By the rude bridge that arched the flood,
Their flag to April's breeze unfurled;
Here once the embattled farmers stood;
And fired the shot heard round the world.
The foe long since in silence slept;
Alike the conqueror silent sleeps,
And time the ruined bridge has swept,
Down the dark stream that seaward creeps.
On this green bank, by this soft stream,
We place with joy a votive stone,
That memory may their deeds redeem,
When, like our sires, our sons are gone.
O Thou who made those heroes dare,
To die, and leave their children free,
Bid time and nature gently spare,
The shaft we raised to them and Thee.

Less than two months after the Battles of Lexington and Concord, on June 12, 1775, the Continental Congress, under President John Hancock, declared:

> Congress...considering the present critical, alarming and calamitous state...do earnestly recommend, that Thursday, the 12th of July next, be observed by the inhabitants of all the English Colonies on this Continent, as a Day of Public Humiliation, Fasting and Prayer,
>
> that we may with united hearts and voices, unfeignedly confess and deplore our many sins
>
> and offer up our joint supplications to the All-wise, Omnipotent and merciful Disposer of all Events, humbly beseeching Him to forgive our iniquities...
>
> It is recommended to Christians of all denominations to assemble for public worship and to abstain from servile labor and recreations of said day.

The conflict was now underway that in eight years would end in American independence.

———⪧•⪦———

5.
BATTLE OF BUNKER HILL

"Don't shoot until you see the whites of their eyes!" was the order given June 17, 1775, by Colonel William Prescott. He was commanding the troops on Breed's Hill, adjacent Bunker Hill, which guarded the north entrance to Boston Harbor.

Providentially for the Americans, this being the first naval engagement of the war, the British had the wrong size cannon balls on their ships and therefore were unable to effectively bombard the American position.

British General William Howe had to disembark 2,300 British soldiers and charge them up the hill with bayonets fixed. Twice the Americans repelled them, forcing them back down the hill, until the Americans ran out of gunpowder. The British then took the hill, and burned the nearby town of Charlestown.

In this first action of war, the Continental Army saw over 1,000 British casualties and nearly 500 American deaths.

The same day, 300 miles away in Philadelphia, the Continental Congress drafted George Washington's commission as Commander-in-Chief, for which he refused a salary.

Washington wrote to his wife, Martha:

Dearest...It has been determined in Congress, that the whole army raised for the defense of the American Cause shall be put under my care, and that it is necessary for me to proceed immediately to Boston to take... command... I shall rely therefore, confidently, on that Providence which has heretofore preserved, and been bountiful to me...

I...got Colonel Pendleton to Draft a Will...the Provision made for you, in case of my death, will, I hope, be agreeable.

General Washington rode to Boston and took command. Shortly after, Georgia's Provincial Congress passed a motion July 5, 1775:

That this Congress apply to his Excellency the Governor...requesting him to appoint a Day of Fasting and Prayer throughout this Province, on account of the disputes subsisting between America and the Parent State.

On July 7, 1775, Georgia's Provincial Governor replied:

> Gentlemen: I have taken the...request made by...a Provincial Congress, and must premise, that I cannot consider that meeting as constitutional; but as the request is expressed in such loyal and dutiful terms, and the ends proposed being such as every good man must most ardently wish for, I will certainly appoint a Day of Fasting and Prayer to be observed throughout this Province. Jas. Wright.

Of the Continental Congress passing a Day of Public Humiliation, Fasting and Prayer, John Adams wrote to his wife, Abigail, July 12, 1775:

> We have appointed a Continental fast. Millions will be upon their knees at once before their great Creator, imploring His forgiveness and blessing; His smiles on American Council and arms.

On July 19, 1775, the Journals of the Continental Congress recorded:

> Agreed, That the Congress meet here tomorrow morning, at half

after 9 o'clock, in order to attend divine service at Mr. Duche's Church; and that in the afternoon they meet here to go from this place and attend divine service at Doctor Allison's church.

As the Revolutionary War began, Connecticut Governor Jonathan Trumbull wrote to General George Washington, July 13, 1775:

> The Honorable Congress have proclaimed a Fast to be observed by the inhabitants of all the English Colonies on this continemt, to stand before the Lord in one day, with public humiliation, fasting and prayer, to deplore our many sins, to offer up our joint supplications to God...
>
> They have...appointed you to the high station you possess. The Supreme Director of all events hath cause a wonderful union of hearts and counsels to subsist among us.
>
> Now, therefore, be strong and very courageous. May the God of the armies of Israel shower down the blessings of his Divine Providence on you, give you wisdom and fortitude, cover your head in the day of battle and danger, add success, convince our enemies of their mistaken measures.

6.
CANNONS AND VIOLENT STORMS MAKE BRITISH EVACUATE BOSTON

"In the Name of the Great Jehovah and the Continental Congress" shouted Ethan Allen, May 10, 1775, when asked by the surprised British commander of Fort Ticonderoga in whose name his surrender was being demanded. Seven months later, December 1, 1775, 43-year-old General George Washington sent 25-year-old Colonel Henry Knox to bring Fort Ticonderoga's cannons to Boston.

The British had occupied Boston since the Battle of Bunker Hill, blockading the harbor and starving the inhabitants into submission. Henry Knox, who had witnessed the Boston Massacre and the destruction of his bookseller's shop, fled the city with his young wife Lucy.

Knox embarked on his task to move 59 cannons over 300 miles in 3 months from Fort Ticonderoga to Boston - an accomplishment so extraordinary that historian Victor Brooks called it "one of the most stupendous feats of logistics."

Knox and his men arrived at Fort Ticonderoga, where Lake Champlain connects to Lake George, and put the cannons on big flat-bottomed boats. They rowed them in freezing weather to the southern end of Lake George, then dragged them on sleds across the snow. Knox wrote to Washington, December 17, 1775:

> I have had made 42 exceedingly strong sleds and have provided 80 yoke of oxen to drag them as far as Springfield where I shall get fresh cattle to carry them... I hope in 16 or 17 days to be able to present your Excellency a noble train of artillery.

They arrived at the Hudson River, but the ice was not thick enough to support the sleds and one sank. On January 8, 1776, Knox wrote in his diary of help provided by local farmers and pastors:

> Went on the ice about 8 o'clock in the morning and proceeded so carefully that before night we got over 23 sleds and were so lucky as to get the cannon out of the River, owing to the assistance the good people of the city of Albany gave.

Knox arrived at Cambridge, Massachusetts, and on the night of March 4th, with a diversionary attack made to distract the British, Washington's men wrapped wagon wheels with straw to muffle the noise and frantically moved the cannons up to a strategic point on Dorchester Heights overlooking Boston Harbor. To make it appear even more impressive, they painted some logs to look like cannons.

The next morning, March 5, 1776, an astonished British General William Howe looked up at Dorchester Heights and remarked:

> The rebels did more in one night than my whole army would have done in one month.

On March 6, 1776, from his Cambridge Headquarters, General Washington ordered:

> Thursday, the 7th...being set apart by this Province as a Day of Fasting, Prayer and Humiliation,
> "to implore the Lord and Giver of all victory to pardon our manifold sins and wickedness, and that it would please

Him to bless the Continental army with His divine favor and protection," all officers and soldiers are strictly enjoined to pay all due reverence and attention on that day to the sacred duties due to the Lord of hosts for His mercies already received,

and for those blessings which our holiness and uprightness of life can alone encourage us to hope through His mercy to obtain.

On March 7, 1776, General William Howe had planned to attack the Americans by landing 3,000 troops and charging up Dorchester Heights, but a violent snowstorm arose causing the sea to be so turbulent the attack had to be abandoned. General Washington wrote his brother, John Augustine Washington, March 31, 1776:

Upon their discovery of the works next morning, great preparations were made for attacking them; but not being ready before the afternoon, and the weather getting very tempestuous, much blood was saved and a very important blow...prevented.

That this most remarkable Interposition of Providence is for some wise purpose, I have not a doubt.

On March 8, 1776, General Howe sent word to Washington that if the British were allowed to leave Boston unmolested, they would not set fire to the city on their way out. Eight days passed, and on March 16, 1776, the Continental Congress approved without dissent a resolution by General William Livingston:

Congress....desirous...to have people of all ranks and degrees duly impressed with a solemn sense of God's superintending providence, and of their duty, devoutly to rely...on his aid and direction...

do earnestly recommend...a Day of Humiliation, Fasting and Prayer; that we may, with united hearts, confess and bewail our manifold sins and transgressions, and, by sincere repentance and amendment of life, appease God's righteous displeasure,

Cannons and Violent Storms Make British Evacuate Bostons

and, through the merits and mediation of Jesus Christ, obtain His pardon and forgiveness.

On March 17, 1776, British General Howe finally gave the order to all his troops to board their ships and together with about a thousand British loyalists, including the parents of Henry Knox's wife, the British evacuated Boston.

With enthusiasm high, General Washington put out a desparate plea for reinforcements.

Connecticut Governor Jonathan Trumbull responded August of 1776, by putting out an appeal for nine more regiments of volunteers, stating:

In this day of calamity, to trust altogether to the justice of our cause, without our utmost exertion, would be tempting Providence...

March on!- This shall be your warrant: Play the man for God, and for the cities of our God. May the Lord of Hosts, the God of the Armies of Israel, be your Captain, your Leader, your Conductor, and Saviour.

7.
DENSE FOG APPEARS,
ALLOWING 8,000 TROOPS TO ESCAPE

With Boston freed from British occupation, New York was the next target.

Washington's ranks swelled to 20,000 as he fortified Brooklyn Heights. Citizens in New York pulled down the statue of King Geoege and classes were suspended at King's College, which was later renamed Columbia University. Anxeity mounted, though, as the British assembled the largest invasion force in world history to that date. - 32,000 troops on over 400 ships. The thousands of wooden masts in New York's harbor looked like a forest of trees. Washington wrote to his younger brother, John Augustine Washington, May 31, 1776:

> We expect a very bloody summer of it at New York... We are not either in men, or arms, prepared for it... If our cause is just, as I do most religiously believe it to be, the same Providence which has in many instances appear'd for us, will strill go on to afford its aid.

General George Washington ordered, May 15, 1776:

The Continental Congress having ordered Friday the 17th instant to be observed as a Day of Fasting, Humiliation and Prayer, humbly to supplicate the mercy of Almighty God, that it would please Him to pardon all our manifold sins and transgressions, and to prosper the arms of the United Colonies, and finally establish the peace and freedom of America upon a solid and lasting foundation;

The General commands all officers and soldiers to pay strict obedience to the orders of the Continental Congress; that, by their unfeigned and pious observance of their religious duties, they may incline the Lord and Giver of victory to prosper our arms.

On July 9, 1776, Washington's men were encouraged when messengers from Philadelphia brought a copy of the recently passed Declaration of Independence. Washington had it read out loud to his troops. It acknowledged God four times:

Laws of Nature and of **Nature's God**...All men are created equal, that they are endowed by their **Creator** with certain unalienable rights...
Appealing to the **Supreme Judge of the World** for the rectitude of our intentions...Firm reliance on the protection of **divine Providence.**

Washington expected the British to attack from the sea as they did at the Battle of Bunker Hill. Instead, 10,000 British troops landed a distance from New York and a British loyalist led them through Jamaica Pass, marching all night long to make a surprise attack on the Continental Army from behind on August 27, 1776. An estimated 3,000 Americans were killed or wounded compared to only 392 British casualties. The Battle of Brooklyn Heights was the first major battle after America had declared its independence and it was the largest battle of the entire war.

As General Washington watched 400 brave soldiers of the First Maryland Regiment charge six times to their deaths directly into the British lines, allowing the rest of the Continental Army to find cover, he exclaimed:

"Good God, what brave fellows I have lost this day."

British General Howe trapped the American troops on Brooklyn Heights with their backs against the sea. That night, Washington made the desperate decision to evacuate his entire army by ferrying it across the East River to Manhattan Island. The sea was boisterous where the British ships were, but providentially calm in the East River allowing Washington's boats to transport troops, horses and cannons.

As the sun began to rise, half of the American troops were still in danger, but a 'miraculously' thick fog lingered blocking the evacuation from being seen by the British.

Major Ben Tallmadge, Washington's Chief of Intelligence, wrote:

> As the dawn of the next day approached, those of us who remained in the trenches became very anxious for our own safety, and when the dawn appeared there were several regiments still on duty.
>
> At this time a very dense fog began to rise off the river, and it seemed to settle in a peculiar manner over both encampments.
>
> I recollect this peculiar providential occurrence perfectly well, and so very dense was the atmosphere that I could scarcely discern a man at six yards distance...We tarried until the sun had risen, but the fog remained as dense as ever.

General Washington was on the last boat that left Brooklyn Heights. The British never again had such an opportunity to capture the entire American army at one time.

Had the Americans not been able to evacuate, they would have been captured and Washington would have been hung.

America would have continued as just another colony in Britain's expanding global empire, along with India, Kenya, Egypt, South Africa and Australia.

General George Washington wrote: August 20, 1778:

Undergoing the strangest vicissitudes that perhaps ever attended any one contest since the creation....the Hand of Providence has been so conspicuous in all this - the course of the war - that he must be worse than an infidel that lacks faith...

But it will be time enough for me to turn Preacher when my present appointment ceases.

8.

IN THEIR LOWEST STATE, WASHINGTON "INSPIRED BY HEAVEN" LEADS TO VICTORY

After the amazing evacuation from Brooklyn Heights, Washington sought to know British plans, so 21-year-old Nathan Hale volunteered as a spy. He was caught and hung. His last words were: "I only regret that I have but one life to lose for my country."

The Continental Army was chased out of New York, across New Jersey, and into Pennsylvania. In six months, ranks dwindled from 20,000 to 2,000 exhausted soldiers who were planning to leave at year's end, as they had only enlisted for six months.

Philadelphia was in panic, expecting a British invasion. The Continental Congress packed up and fled, giving their last instruction: "...until Congress shall otherwise order, General Washington shall be possessed of full power to order and direct all things."

Washington had Thomas Paine's pamphlet, "The American Crisis," read to his troops:

These are the times that try men's souls. The summer soldier and the sunshine patriot will, in this crisis, shrink from the service of their country...Tyranny, like hell, is not easily conquered; yet we have this consolation with us, that the harder the conflict, the more glorious the triumph...Heaven knows how to put a proper price upon its goods; and it would be strange indeed if so celestial an article as FREEDOM should not be highly rated...

In the 15th century the whole English army...was driven back...by a few broken forces...headed by a woman, Joan of Arc...Would that Heaven might inspire some Jersey maid to spirit up her countrymen...

With the password for his military operation being "Victory or Death," Washington's troops crossed the ice-filled Delaware River on Christmas Day evening in a blizzard. Trudging through blinding snow, with one soldier freezing to death on the march, they attacked Trenton, New Jersey, at daybreak, December 26, 1776.

The feared German Hessian mercenary troops hired by King George III were trained to fight in an open field, and were not prepared for Americans firing from behind every tree. The Americans captured nearly a thousand in just over an hour, with only a few wounded, one being James Monroe, the future 5th President.

After winning the Battle of Trenton, British General Cornwallis sent his 8,000-man British army to attack Washington near Princeton, New Jersey. The night before the battle, Washington left his campfires burning and silently marched his army around the back of the British camp at Princeton. At daybreak, January 3, 1777, Washington attacked. At one point, American troops under John Cadwalader retreated. General Washington quickly rode over, stopped the retreat, then rode ahead of his troops to within thirty yards of the British. Turning and facing his men, he yelled "halt," then "fire." The British returned fire, filling the field with smoke. Many thought Washington was surely shot, being exposed to fire from both sides, but when the air cleared, Washington appeared, waving his men forward. Three British regiments were captured. Enthusiasm swept America.

Frederick the Great of Prussia called the ten days from December 26, 1776 to January 3, 1777, "the most brilliant in the world's history." Yale President Ezra Stiles stated in an Election Address before Connecticut General Assembly:

> In our lowest and most dangerous estate...we sustained ourselves against the British Army of 60,000 troops, commanded by...the ablest generals Britain could procure throughout Europe, with a naval force of 22,000 seamen in above 80 men-of-war...Independence...was sealed and confirmed by God Almighty in the victory of General Washington at Trenton, and in the surprising movement and battle of Princeton...Who but a Washington, inspired by Heaven, could have struck out the great movement and maneuver of Princeton?...The United States are under peculiar obligations to become a holy people unto the Lord our God.

9.
VICTORY OF SARATOGA

Her beautiful, long hair was scalped off her head by Indians after she was shot. This was the fate of Jane McCrea, whose loyalist fiancé David Jones had only weeks earlier joined British General "Gentleman Johnny" Burgoyne, who in June of 1777, was marching with 7,000 troops from Canada to Albany, New York.

Recapturing Fort Ticonderoga, Burgoyne headed down the Hudson River Valley, making a treaty with the Mohawk Tribe to terrorize American settlements.

When Indians returned to camp with a scalp of beautiful long hair, David Jones instantly recognized it as his fiancée's. The resulting outrage forced Burgoyne to tell the Indians to show restraint. Insulted, the Indians left Burgoyne stranded deep in the forest.

Jane McCrea's death, later immortalized in James Fenimore Cooper's novel, *The Last of the Mohicans*, rallied Americans, causing ranks to swell to 15,000. The British tried to send reinforcements, but were prevented, as Yale President Ezra Stiles explained, May 8, 1783:

> To whom but the Ruler of the Winds shall we ascribe it, that the
> British reinforcement, in the summer of 1777, was delayed on the ocean

three months by contrary winds, until it was too late for the conflagrating General Clinton to raise the siege of Saratoga.

At the Battle of Saratoga, October 7, 1777, General Benedict Arnold led a valiant charge on the British flank, resulting in him being considered the hero of the battle. Shortly thereafter, October 17, 1777, British General Johnny Burgoyne surrendered to American General Horatio Gates, and over 6,000 British troops were captured.

When news of Burgoyne's surrender reached King Louis XVI in France, he decided to join the American cause, which turned the Revolution into a global war and stretched Britain's resources around the world, including the West Indies and Europe.

The surrender of Burgoyne at Saratoga is considered a major turning point in the Revolution and one of the most important battles in world history. Artist John Trumbull's painting of the Surrender of General Burgoyne is in the U.S. Capitol Rotunda. General George Washington wrote to his brother John Augustine the day after the victory:

> I most devoutly congratulate my country, and every well-wisher to the cause, on this signal stroke of Providence.

In gratefulness for the victory of Saratoga, the Continental Congress, on November 1, 1777, proclaimed the first National Day of Thanksgiving, stating:

> That with one heart and one voice the good people may express

the grateful feeling of their hearts...join the penitent confession of their manifold sins...that it may please God, through the merits of Jesus Christ, mercifully to forgive and blot them out of rememberance...and...under the providence of Almighty God...secure for these United States the greatest of all human blessings, independence and peace.

Signer of the Declaration Roger Sherman of Connecticut, when he heard of the victory of Saratoga, exclaimed: "This is the Lord's doing, and marvelous in our eyes!"

10.
WINTER AT VALLEY FORGE

After the American victory at Saratoga, British General Howe struck back by driving the patriots out of Philadelphia. While 11,000 Americans died on British starving ships, another 11,000 soldiers set up camp, December 19, 1777, at Valley Forge, just 25 miles from Philadelphia. Soldiers were from every State in the new union, ages 12 to 60, white, African American and even American Indian. Over 2,500 died at the rate of 12 per day from freezing exposure, hunger and disease. A Committee from Congress reported: "Feet and legs froze till they became black, and it was often necessary to amputate them." Lutheran Pastor Henry Muhlenberg, whose sons Peter and Frederick were in the First U.S. Congress, wrote in *The Notebook of a Colonial Clergyman:*

> I heard a fine example today, namely, that His Excellency General Washington rode around among his army yesterday and admonished each and every one to fear God, to put away the wickedness...and to practice the Christian virtues...God has...marvelously, preserved him from harm in the midst of countless perils, ambuscades, fatigues.

On December 24, 1983, President Ronald Reagan stated in a Radio Address:

> The image of George Washington kneeling in prayer in the snow is one of the most famous in American history.

Hessian Major Carl Leopold Baurmeister noted the only thing that kept the American army from disintegrating was their "spirit of liberty." In February, 1778, Prussian Officer Baron von Steuben arrived to train and drill the American volunteers, transforming them into an army. On April 21, 1778, Washington wrote to Lt. Col. John Banister:

> No history...can furnish an instance of an army's suffering such uncommon hardships as ours has done, and bearing them with the same patience and fortitude -
>
> To see men without clothes to cover their nakedness, without blankets to lay on, without shoes, by which their marches might be traced by the blood from their feet, and almost as often without provisions...marching through frost and snow, and at Christmas taking up their winter quarters within a day's march of the enemy, without a house or hut to cover them...and submitting to it without a murmur, is a mark of patience and obedience which in my opinion can scarce be paralleled.

Successfully keeping the army intact through the devastating winter, Washington issued the order from Valley Forge, April 12, 1778:

> The Honorable Congress having thought proper to recommend to the United States of America to set apart Wednesday, the 22nd inst., to be observed as a day of Fasting, Humiliation and Prayer, that at one time, and with one voice, the righteous dispensations of Providence may be acknowledged, and His goodness and mercy towards our arms supplicated and implored: The General directs that the day shall be most religiously observed in the Army; that no work shall be done thereon, and that the several chaplains do prepare discourses.

On May 2, 1778, Washington ordered:

> The Commander-in-Chief directs that Divine service be performed every Sunday...To the distinguished character of Patriot, it should be our highest Glory to laud the more distinguished Character of Christian.

11.
TREACHEROUS SCHEME OF BENEDICT ARNOLD EXPOSED JUST IN TIME

"Enemies foreign and domestic." General Benedict Arnold was one of the most popular leaders in America. He was a national hero for capturing Fort Ticonderoga with Ethan Allen, and for leading the daring charge against the British at the Battle of Saratoga.

Benedict Arnold's wife, though, was a loyalist to Britain. She began to hint to Benedict that the Americans did not sufficiently appreciate him. By the end of 1779, she began to make contact with a British spy in Philadelphia, Major John Andre.

Meanwhile, the Continental Congress declared a Day of Prayer, which Virginia Governor Thomas Jefferson chose to observe, signing a Proclamation of Prayer, November 11, 1779:

> Congress...hath thought proper...to recommend to the several States...a
> day of public and solemn Thanksgiving to Almighty God, for his mercies,
> and of Prayer, for the continuance of his favour...That He would go forth
> with our hosts and crown our arms with victory; That He would grant

to His church, the plentiful effusions of Divine Grace, and pour out His Holy Spirit on all Ministers of the Gospel; That He would bless and prosper the means of education, and spread the light of Christian knowledge through the remotest corners of the earth...

I do therefore...issue this proclamation...appointing...a day of public and solemn thanksgiving and prayer to Almighty God...Given under by hand...this 11th day of November, in the year of our Lord, 1779...Thomas Jefferson.

The next spring, General Washington issued the order from his headquarters at Morristown, April 6, 1780:

Congress having been pleased by their Proclamation of the 11th of last month to appoint Wednesday the 22nd instant to be set apart and observed as a day of Fasting, Humiliation and Prayer...there should be no labor or recreations on that day.

On August 30, 1780, General Benedict Arnold made his decision. He conspired with British General Henry Clinton to surrender West Point for 20,000 pounds, equivalent to one million dollars today. West Point was a fort which controlled the Hudson River Valley, extending from near Canada in the North to New York City in the south, thereby dividing colonial America in half, with the New England Colonies on the east and Middle and Southern Colonies on the west.

The British spy, Major John Andre, met with General Benedict Arnold. He then tried to return to the British lines dressed as a civilian. The American sentries stopped him and searched him once, twice, and then, just before letting him pass, they decided to search his boots. There, in a hollowed out space in the heel of the boot, they found the map of West Point with instructions revealing where to attack.

The American sentries arrested Andre and marched him back into the office of General Benedict Arnold. Realizing that his plan was about to be revealed, Arnold escaped on the ship *Vulture*. British Major John Andre was executed as a spy.

Washington wrote September 26, 1780:

Treason of the blackest dye was yesterday discovered! General Arnold who commanded at West Point, lost to every sentiment of honor - of public and private obligations - was about to deliver up that important post into the hands of the enemy. Such an event must have given the American cause a deadly wound if not fatal stab.

Happily the treason has been timely discovered to prevent the fatal misfortune. The providential train of circumstances which led to it affords the most convincing proof that the Liberties of America are the object of divine Protection.

Yale President Ezra Stiles stated, May 8, 1783:

A providential miracle detected the conspiracy of Arnold, even in the critical moment of the execution of that infernal plot, in which the body of the American army, then at West Point, with his excellency General Washington himself, were to have been rendered into the hands of the enemy!

The Continental Congress issued a Day of Thanksgiving, October 18, 1780:

In the late remarkable interposition of His watchful providence, in the rescuing the person of our Commander-in-Chief and the army from imminent dangers, at the moment when treason was ripened for execution...it is therefore recommended...a Day of Public Thanksgiving and Prayer...to confess our unworthiness...and to offer fervent supplications to the God of all grace...to cause the knowledge of Christianity to spread over all the earth.

12.
RIVER WATERS RISE MIRACULOUSLY AND STOP ROYAL ARMY

The Battle of Cowpens, January 17, 1781, depicted in the movie *The Patriot*, involved American General Daniel Morgan having a line of militia fire into the advancing forces of British General Cornwallis, which consisted of Colonel Banastre Tarleton's dragoons, British Regulars, Highlanders and loyalists.

When the Americans hastily retreated over a hill, British Colonel Tarleton, known as "The Butcher," gave into the temptation to pursue, only to be surprised by American Continentals waiting over the other side, firing at point-blank range.

In the confusion, 110 British were killed and 830 captured. The Battle of Cowpens is widely considered the tactical masterpiece and turning point of the war.

After the battle, General Daniel Morgan made a hasty retreat north toward Virginia, meeting up with American General Nathaniel Greene. Cornwallis regrouped and chased the Americans as fast as he could, discarding heavy equipment and supplies along the way.

Cornwallis arrived at the Catawba River just two hours after the Americans had crossed, but a sudden storm made the river impassable, delaying the British pursuit. The British nearly overtook the Americans at the Yadkin River, but again rains flooded the river slowing the British. Now it was a race to the Dan River. General Nathaniel Greene quickly led the Americans across before another flash flood blocked the British.

British Commander Henry Clinton wrote:

> Here the royal army was again stopped by a sudden rise of the waters, which had only just fallen (almost miraculously) to let the enemy over, who could not else have eluded Lord Cornwallis' grasp, so close was he upon their rear.

In March of 1781, General Washington wrote to William Gordon:

We have...abundant reasons to thank Providence for its many favorable interpositions in our behalf. It has at times been my only dependence, for all other resources seemed to have failed us.

Having discarded his supplies in the chase, Cornwallis was ordered by British General Henry Clinton to move his 8,000 troops to where the York River entered Chesapeake Bay and wait for British ships. French King Louis XVI, having been persuaded by Ben Franklin and Marquis de Lafayette, sent ships and troops to help the Americans. French Admiral de Grasse left off fighting the British in the West Indies and sailed 24 ships to the mouth of Chesapeake Bay, where, in the Battle of the Capes, he drove off 19 British ships which were trying to evacuate Cornwallis' men.

De Grasse's 3,000 French troops and General Rochambeau's 6,000 French troops hurriedly joined General Lafayette's division as they marched to help Washington trap Cornwallis against the sea. They joined the troops of Generals Benjamin Lincoln, Baron von Steuben, Modecai Gist, Henry Knox and John Peter Muhlenberg.

Altogether, 17,000 French and American troops surrounded Cornwallis, forcing him to surrender on October 19, 1781. Yale President Ezra Stiles wrote, May 8, 1783:

Who but God could have ordained the critical arrival of the Gallic (French) fleet, so as to...assist...in the siege...of Yorktown?... Should we not...ascribe to a Supreme energy...the wise...generalship displayed by General

Greene...leaving the...roving Cornwallis to pursue his helter-skelter ill fated march into Virginia... It is God who had raised up for us a...powerful ally...a chosen army and a naval force: who sent us a Rochambeau...to fight side by side with a Washington...in the...battle of Yorktown.

General Washington wrote October 20, 1781:

To diffuse the general Joy through every breast the General orders...Divine Service to be performed tomorrow in the several Brigades...Troops not on duty should universally attend with that gratitude of heart which the recognition of such astonishing Interposition of Providence demands.

On October 11, 1782, the Congress of the Confederation passed:

It being the indispensable duty of all nations...to offer up their supplications to Almighty God...the United States in Congress assembled...do hereby recommend it to the inhabitants of these states in general, to observe...the last Thursday...of November next, as a Day of Solemn Thanksgiving to God for all his mercies.

On September 3, 1783, the Revolutionary War officially ended with the Treaty of Paris, signed by Ben Franklin, John Adams, John Jay and David Hartley:

In the name of the Most Holy and Undivided Trinity. It having pleased the Divine Providence to dispose the hearts of the most serene and most potent Prince George the Third, by the Grace of God, King of Great Britain...and of the United States of America, to forget all past misunderstandings and differences... Done at Paris, this third day of September, in the year of our Lord one thousand seven hundred and eighty-three.

Ronald Reagan proclaimed a Day of Prayer, January 27, 1983, stating:

In 1775, the Continental Congress proclaimed the first National Day of Prayer... In 1783, the Treaty of Paris officially ended the long, weary Revolutionary War during which a National Day of Prayer had been proclaimed every spring for eight years.

George Washington wrote to General Nathanael Greene, February 6, 1783:

It will not be believed that such a force as Great Britain has employed for eight years in this country could be baffled in their plan of subjugating it by numbers infinitely less, composed of men oftentimes half starved; always in rags, without pay, and experiencing, at times, every species of distress which human nature is capable of undergoing.

Washington added in his Farewell Orders, November 2, 1783:

The singular interpositions of Providence in our feeble condition were such, as could scarcely escape the attention of the most unobserving; while the perseverance of the Armies of the United States, through almost every possible suffering and discouragement for the space of eight long years, was little short of a standing miracle.

With the war over, Massachusetts Governor John Hancock proclaimed, November 8, 1783:

The Citizens of these United States have every Reason for Praise and Gratitude to the God of their salvation...

I do...appoint...the 11th day of December next (the day recommended by the Congress to all the States) to be religiously observed as a Day of Thanksgiving and Prayer, that all the people may then assemble to celebrate...that He hath been pleased to continue to us the Light of the Blessed Gospel...

That we also offer up fervent supplications...to cause pure Religion and Virtue to flourish...and to fill the world with His glory.

13.
WHEN LEADERS OF ALL DENOMINATIONS PRAYED TOGETHER

On February 21, 1786, New Hampshire's Governor John Langdon set a Day of Fasting:

That He would be pleased to bless the great Council of the United States of America and direct their deliberations...that he would rain down righteousness upon the earth, revive religion, and spread abroad the knowledge of the true God, the Saviour of man.

At the Constitutional Convention, 1787, the 55 writers of the U.S. Constitution were:

26 Episcopalian Christians
11 Presbyterian Christians
7 Congregationalist Christians
2 Lutheran Christians
2 Dutch Reformed Christians

2 Methodist Christians
2 Quaker Christians
2 Roman Catholic Christians
and Dr. Franklin, who called for prayer at the Constitutional Convention, June 28, 1787, stating:

In the beginning of the contest with Great Britain, when we were sensible of danger, we had daily prayer in this room for the divine protection.- Our prayers, Sir, were heard and they were graciously answered. All of us who were engaged in the struggle must have observed frequent instances of a superintending providence in our favor... I have lived, Sir, a long time, and the longer I live, the more convincing proofs I see of this truth - that God Governs in the affairs of men. And if a sparrow cannot fall to the ground without His notice, is it probable that an empire can rise without His aid? We have been assured, Sir, in the Sacred Writings, that 'except the Lord build the House, they labor in vain that build it.'...

I also believe that without his concurring aid we shall succeed in this political building no better than the Builders of Babel...I therefore beg leave to move-that henceforth prayers imploring the assistance of Heaven, and its blessing on our deliberations, be held in this Assembly every morning before we proceed to business.

The Constitution went into effect June 21, 1788, when 2/3's of the States ratified it:

DELAWARE - 1st to ratify the U.S. Constitution, stated in its **1776 State Constitution**: "Every person...appointed to any office...shall...subscribe...'I...profess faith in GOD THE FATHER, and in JESUS CHRIST His only Son, and in the HOLY GHOST, one God, blessed for evermore; and I do acknowledge the Holy Scriptures of the Old and New Testament to be given by Divine inspiration.'"

PENNSYLVANIA - 2nd to ratify the U.S. Constitution, stated in its **1776 State Constitution**, signed by Ben Franklin: "Each member, before he takes his seat, shall...subscribe...'I do believe in one GOD, the Creator and Governor of the Universe, the Rewarder of the good and the Punisher of the wicked. And I do acknowledge the Scriptures of the Old and New Testament to be given by Divine Inspiration.'"

 NEW JERSEY - 3rd to ratify the U.S. Constitution, stated in its **1776 State Constitution**: "All persons, professing a belief in the faith of any PROTESTANT sect, who shall demean themselves peaceably under the government...shall be capable of being elected."

 GEORGIA - 4th to ratify the U.S. Constitution, stated in its **1777 State Constitution**: "Representatives shall be chosen out of the residents in each county...and they shall be of the PROTESTANT religion."

 CONNECTICUT - 5th to ratify the U.S. Constitution, retained its **1662 Colonial Constitution**, which was established PROTESTANT CONGREGATIONAL, till 1818: "By the Providence of GOD...having from their ancestors derived a free and excellent Constitution...whereby the legislature depends on the free and annual election...The free fruition of such liberties and privileges as humanity, civility and CHRISTIANITY call for."

 MASSACHUSETTS - 6th to ratify the U.S. Constitution, stated in its **1780 State Constitution,** written by John Adams: "Any person...before he...execute the duties of his...office...[shall] subscribe...'I...declare, that I believe the CHRISTIAN religion, and have a firm persuasion of its truth'....The legislature shall...authorize the support and maintenance of public PROTESTANT teachers of piety, religion and morality."

MARYLAND - 7th to ratify the U.S. Constitution, stated in its **1776 State Constitution**: "No other test...ought to be required, on admission to any office...than such oath of support and fidelity to this State...and a declaration of a belief in the CHRISTIAN religion."

SOUTH CAROLINA - 8th to ratify the U.S. Constitution, stated in its **1778 State Constitution**: "No person shall be eligible to a seat...unless he be of the PROTESTANT religion...The CHRISTIAN PROTESTANT religion shall be deemed...the established religion of this State."

NEW HAMPSHIRE - 9th to ratify the U.S. Constitution, stated in its **1784 State Constitution**: "No person shall be capable of being elected...who is not of the PROTESTANT religion."

VIRGINIA - 10th to ratify the U.S. Constitution, stated in its **1776 State Constitution**, Bill of Rights, written by James Madison and George Mason: "It is the mutual duty of all to practice CHRISTIAN forbearance, love, and charity towards each other."

NEW YORK - 11th to ratify the U.S. Constitution, stated in its **1777 State Constitution**: "The United American States...declare...'Laws of nature and of NATURE'S GOD...All men are created equal; that they are endowed by their CREATOR with certain unalienable rights...Appealing to the SUPREME JUDGE of the world...A firm reliance on the protection of DIVINE PROVIDENCE'...People of this State, ordain...the free exercise and enjoyment of religious profession and worship, without discrimination...Provided, That the liberty of conscience, hereby granted, shall not be so construed as to excuse acts of licentiousness."

 NORTH CAROLINA - 12th to ratify the U.S. Constitution, stated in its **1776 State Constitution**: "No person, who shall deny the being of GOD or the truth of the PROTESTANT religion, or the Divine authority either of the Old or New Testaments, or who shall hold religious principles incompatible with the freedom and safety of the State, shall be capable of holding...office."

 RHODE ISLAND - 13th to ratify the U.S. Constitution, retained its 1663 **Colonial Constitution** till 1843, which stated: "By the blessing of God...a full liberty in religious concernements...rightly grounded upon GOSPEL principles, will give the best and greatest security...in the true CHRISTIAN faith and worship of God...They may...defend themselves, in their just rights and liberties against all the enemies of the CHRISTIAN faith.

U.S. Supreme Court Justice Hugo Lafayette Black wrote in *Engel v. Vitale*, 1962:

> As late as the time of the Revolutionary War, there were established Churches in at least 8 of the 13 former colonies and established religions in at least 4 of the other 5.

John K. Wilson wrote in Religion Under the State Constitutions 1776-1800 (*Journal of Church and State*, Volume 32, Autumn 1990, Number 4, pp. 754):

> An establishment of religion, in terms of direct tax aid to Churches, was the situation in 9 of the 13 colonies on the eve of the American revolution.

The Journal of the U.S. House recorded that on March 27, 1854, the 33rd Congress voted unanimously to print Rep. James Meacham's report, which stated:

> At the adoption of the Constitution, we believe every State - certainly 10 of the 13 - provided as regularly for the support of the Church as for the support of the Government...Down to the Revolution, every colony did sustain religion in some form. It was deemed peculiarly proper that the religion of liberty should be upheld by a free people...
>
> Had the people, during the Revolution, had a suspicion of any attempt to war against Christianity, that Revolution would have been strangled in its cradle.

The same week Congress passed the Bill of Rights, President Washington declared, October 3, 1789:

> Whereas both Houses of Congress have by their joint Committee requested me "to recommend...a Day of Public Thanksgiving and Prayer to be

observed by acknowledging with grateful hearts the many signal favors of Almighty God, **especially by affording them an opportunity peaceably to establish a form of government for their safety and happiness"**...

I do recommend...the 26th day of November...to be devoted by the People of these United States to the service of that great and glorious Being, who is the beneficent Author of all the good that was, that is, or that will be;

that we may then all unite in rendering unto Him our sincere and humble thanks...for the peaceable and rational manner in which we have been enabled to **establish constitutions of government** for our safety and happiness,

and **particularly the national one now lately instituted**, for the civil and religious liberty with which we are blessed.

MIRACLES IN AMERICAN HISTORY - SUSIE FEDERER

14.
WHEN ADAMS DECLARED
A DAY OF FASTING AND PRAYER

After George Washington's two terms, John Adams was elected the second President.

The situation in France had changed. There was a French Revolution and an atheistic Reign of Terror. In Paris, Robespierre headed up the Committee of Public Safety, which accused, arrested, then beheaded 40,000 of the businessmen, the wealthy, and the royalty, including King Louis XVI and Marie Antoinette.

All churches were closed; religious monuments destroyed; graves desecrated; crosses forbidden; public and private worship and education outlawed; priests and ministers, along with those who harbored them, were executed on sight; all in an intentional campaign to dechristianize French society, replacing it with a civic religion of state worship. Hundreds of thousands were killed throughout France, especially in a religious area called the Vendee.

French privateers ignored treaties and by 1798, had seized nearly 300 American ships bound for British ports. Talleyrand, the French Minister of Foreign Affairs, demanded millions of dollars in bribes in order for them to leave America's ships alone.

Known as the XYZ Affair, the American commission of Charles Pinckney, John Marshall and Elbridge Gerry refused. The cry went out across America, "Millions for defense, not a cent for tribute."

As America and France came close to war, President John Adams asked George Washington, now retired at Mount Vernon, to again be the Commander-in-Chief of the American Army. Washington agreed, writing on July 13, 1798:

Satisfied...you have...exhausted, to the last drop, the cup of reconciliation, we can, with pure hearts, appeal to Heaven for the justice of our cause; and may confidently trust the final result to that kind Providence who has, heretofore, and so often, signally favored the people of these United States...

Feeling how incumbent it is upon every person...to contribute at all times to his country's welfare, and especially in a moment like the present, when everything we hold dear and sacred is so seriously threatened, I have finally determined to accept the commission of Commander-in-Chief.

President Adams declared a Day of Fasting, March 23, 1798, and again, March 6, 1799:

The people of the United States are still held in jeopardy by...insidious acts of a foreign nation, as well as by the dissemination among them of those principles subversive to the foundations of all religious, moral, and social obligations...

I hereby recommend...a Day of Solemn Humiliation, Fasting and Prayer; That the citizens...call to mind our numerous offenses against the Most

High God, confess them before Him with the sincerest penitence, implore His pardoning mercy, through the Great Mediator and Redeemer, for our past transgressions,

and that through the grace of His Holy Spirit, we may be disposed and enabled to yield a more suitable obedience to His righteous requisitions...

"Righteousness exalteth a nation but sin is a reproach to any people."

The prayers of the country were answered, and war with France was averted.

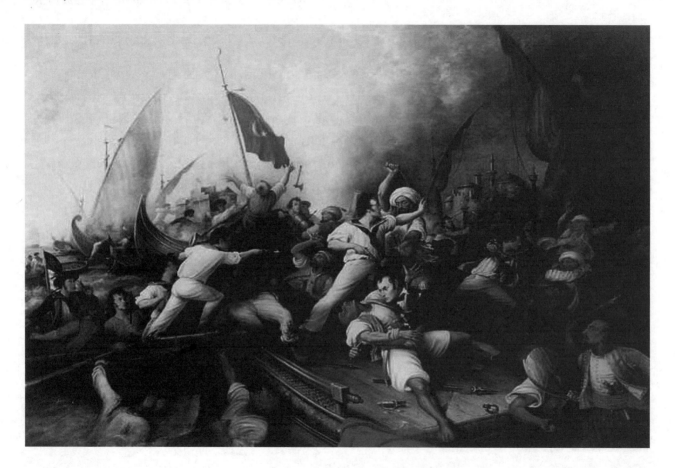

15.
BARBARY PIRATE WARS

Muslims enslaved millions of Africans and Europeans over the centuries. In the Middle Ages, Catholic orders in Europe collected donations and ransomed captives. In 1625, William Bradford wrote of a Pilgrim ship returning to England with dried fish and beaver skins to trade for supplies, when Muslim pirates captured it and enslaved the crew in Morocco.

European countries then paid millions in tribute, with America covered by Britain's. After the Revolution, Muslim pirates demanded the U.S. pay its own. When pirates captured American ships, Jefferson met Tripoli's ambassador in France, then wrote to Congress, 1785:

> The Ambassador answered us that it was...written in their Qur'an, that all nations who should not have acknowledged Islam's authority were sinners, that it was their...duty to make war upon them...and to make slaves of all they could take as prisoners.

Jefferson arranged for John Paul Jones, the Father of the American Navy, to fight the Muslims on the Black Sea for Catherine the Great of Russia.

The U.S. was paying 20 percent of its Federal budget to the Muslim Barbary Pirates. Then, on December 29, 1803, the new 36-gun U.S. frigate *Philadelphia* ran aground on an uncharted sandbar while patrolling off Morocco's coast. The 307 man crew was imprisoned for 18 months.

To prevent this ship from being used by Muslim pirates, Lt. Stephen Decatur sailed his ship, *Intrepid*, into Tripoli's harbor on the night of February 16, 1804, and set the *Philadelphia* ablaze, then escaped amidst fierce enemy fire. It was the "most bold and daring act of the age."

The U.S. Marines later captured Tripoli, freed the prisoners and forced Muslims to sign a treaty. Stephen Decatur wrote: "Algerians were...masters of duplicity, willing to make agreements and break them as they found convenient."

After the First Barbary War, Francis Scott Key published a poem in Boston's *Independent Chronicle*, December 30, 1805, titled "When the Warrior Returns from the Battle Afar," written to the same tune which nine years later he would use for the "Star-Spangled Banner":

> In conflict resistless each toil they endur'd
> Till their foes shrunk dismay'd from the war's desolation:
> And pale beamed the Crescent, its splendor obscur'd
> By the light of the Star-Bangled Flag of our nation.

Where each flaming star gleamed a meteor of war,
And the turban'd head bowed to the terrible glare.
Then mixt with the olive the laurel shall wave
And form a bright wreath for the brow of the brave.

The Barbary Pirate Wars are referred to in the lines of the U.S. Marine Anthem, "From the halls of Montezuma to the shores of Tripoli..."

On December 5, 1815, at the end of the Second Barbary War, President James Madison announced:

> ...the successful termination of the war which had been commenced against the United States by the Regency of Algiers.
>
> The squadron...under Commodore Decatur lost not a moment after its arrival in the Mediterranean in seeking the naval force of the enemy...and succeeded in capturing two of his ships...He hastened to the port of Algiers, where peace was promptly yielded to his victorious force...
>
> A sensibility, in which you will unite, to the happy lot of our country and to the goodness of a superintending Providence, to which we are indebted for it.

16.
CAPTAIN PERRY DECLARES
"THE PRAYERS OF MY WIFE ARE ANSWERED!"

"We have met the enemy and they are ours," exclaimed Oliver Hazard Perry.

The British incited Indians attacks on American settlements and seized American ships, impressings thousands of sailors. This escalated into the War of 1812.

British ships on Lake Erie were sent to resupply Fort Malden in Amherstburg, Ontario, but were blocked by U.S. Captain Oliver Hazard Perry near Put-in-Bay, Ohio.

September 9, 1813, was recommended by President Madison as a Day of Humiliation & Prayer. The next day, September 10, 1813, Perry, with many of his sailors being free Blacks from Ohio, confronted the British squadron, commanded by the one-armed Commodore Robert Barclay, who helped defeat Napoleon's fleet at the Battle of Trafalgar. Strong winds prevented Perry from getting into a safe position, and the long-range British cannons splintered his flagship, *USS Lawrence*, killing many of his crew. Faithful to his battle flag, "DON'T GIVE UP THE SHIP," 28-year-old Perry and his men courageously rowed a half mile through heavy gunfire to the *USS Niagara*.

The wind suddenly changed directions and Perry sailed directly across the British line, firing broadside. After 15 minutes, the smoke cleared to reveal that for the first time in history an entire British squadron had been disabled at once. The British abandoned Fort Malden. U.S. General William Henry Harrison was then able to recapture Detroit, defeating the British and their  Indian ally Shawnee Chief Tecumseh at the Battle of the Thames, October 5, 1813. The Northwest Territory was now secure for America. To sailors on deck Captain Perry remarked: "The prayers of my wife are answered." To the Secretary of the Navy, Perry wrote:

> It has pleased the Almighty to give the arms of the United States a signal victory over their enemies on this lake. The British squadron, consisting of two ships, two brigs, one schooner, and one sloop have this moment surrendered to the force of my command after a sharp conflict.

President James Madison stated in his 5th Annual Message, December 7, 1813:

> It has pleased the Almighty to bless our arms...On Lake Erie, the squadron under the command of Captain Perry having met the British squadron of superior force, a sanguinary conflict ended in the capture of the whole.

17.
MORE BRITISH TROOPS KILLED BY A TORNADO THAN ALL AMERICAN FIREARMS

James Madison, known as the "Chief Architect of the Constitution," wrote many of the Federalist Papers, convincing the States to ratify the Constitution. He introduced the First Amendment in the first session of Congress.

At the onset of the War of 1812, President James Madison proclaimed a Day of Prayer, July 9, 1812, stating:

> I do therefore recommend...rendering the Sovereign of the Universe...public homage...acknowledging the transgressions which might justly provoke His divine displeasure...seeking His merciful forgiveness...and with a reverence for the unerring precept of our holy religion, to do to others as they would require that others should do to them.

The next year, on July 23, 1813, Madison issued another Day of Prayer, referring to:

"religion, that gift of Heaven for the good of man."

On April 6, 1814, Napoleon abdicated in Europe and was exiled to the Island of Elba. This freed up British forces. Nearly 1,000 American vessels were captured and three invasion armies were sent to New York, New Orleans and Washington, D.C.

On August 24, 1814, a force of 4,500 British soldiers marched toward Washington, D.C. In a panic, citizens hastily evacuated. Dolly Madison is credited with saving the Gilbert Stuart portrait of George Washington by having it cut out of its frame. Her carriage was riding out of the city as British Admiral George Cockburn was riding in.

Admiral Cockburn entered the White House, ate dinner, then set it on fire. He had British soldiers sit in the Congressmen's chairs and hold a mock Congress. When he asked who was in favor of burning the Capitol, they yelled, "aye," and proceeded to torch the Capitol, the Treasury, the Patent Office, the Library of Congress and the Navy Yard.

Suddenly, dark clouds rolled in, wind and thunder grew into a "frightening roar," and lightning began striking. A tornado touched down sending debris flying, blowing off roofs, knocking down chimneys and walls on British troops. Two cannons were lifted off the ground and dropped yards away. Violent winds slammed both horse and rider to the ground.

The book, *Washington Weather,* recorded British Admiral George Cockburn exclaiming to a lady:

Great God, Madam! Is this the kind of storm to which you are accustomed in this infernal country?

To which the lady replied:

No, Sir, this is a special interposition of Providence to drive our enemies from our city.

A British historian wrote:

More British soldiers were killed by this stroke of nature than from all the firearms the American troops had mustered in the feeble defense of their city.

As British forces fled, torrential rains fell for two hours, extinguishing the fires. They marched back to their ships with difficulty on roads covered with downed trees only to find two ships blown ashore and others with damaged riggings.

On September 1, 1814, Madison wrote:

The enemy by a sudden incursion has succeeded in invading the capitol of the nation...During their possession... though for a single day only, they wantonly destroyed the public edifices...An occasion which appeals so forcibly to the...patriotic devotion of the American people, none will forget...Independence...is now to be maintained...with the strength and resources which...Heaven has blessed.

Less than 3 months later, Madison proclaimed a National Day of Public Humiliation, Fasting & Prayer to Almighty God on November 16, 1814, stating:

> The two Houses of the National Legislature having by a joint resolution expressed their desire that in the present time of public calamity and war, a day may be recommended to be observed by the people of the United States as a day of public humiliation and fasting and of prayer to Almighty God for the safety and welfare of these States, His blessing on their arms, and a speedy restoration of peace...
>
> of confessing their sins and transgressions, and of strengthening their vows of repentance...that He would be graciously pleased to pardon all their offenses...
>
> I have deemed it proper...to recommend...a day of...humble adoration to the Great Sovereign of the Universe.

18.
STAR-SPANGLED BANNER WRITTEN IN RESPONSE TO MIRACULOUS VICTORY

September 1814, just weeks after the British burned the U.S. Capitol, they attacked Baltimore, Maryland - the third largest city in America. On the way they caught an elderly physician of Upper Marlboro, Dr. William Beanes. The town feared Dr. Beanes would be hanged so they asked a young lawyer, Francis Scott Key, to sail with Colonel John Skinner under a flag of truce to the British flagship *Tonnant* and arrange a prisoner exchange.

Concerned their plans of attacking Baltimore would be discovered, the British placed Francis Scott Key and Colonel Skinner under armed guard aboard the *HMS Surprise*, then on a sloop where they watched for 25 hours as 19 British ships continually bombarded the earthen Fort McHenry with rockets, mortar shells and cannon balls. Providentially, a thunderstorm made the ground so soft that most of the 1,800 cannon balls the British fired sank in the mud instead of exploding.

On the morning of September 14, 1814, "through the dawn's early light," Key saw the flag still flying. Elated, Key penned "The Star-Spangled Banner."

Most people are familiar with the 1st verse, but the 4th verse had a further impact:

O thus be it ever when free men shall stand,
Between their loved home and the war's desolation;
Blest with victory and peace, may the Heaven-rescued land,
Praise the Power that hath made and preserved us a nation!
Then conquer we must, when our cause it is just;
And this be our motto 'IN GOD IS OUR TRUST'!
And the Star Spangled Banner in triumph shall wave,
Over the land of the free and the home of the brave!

On March 22, 1814, Francis Scott Key told the Washington Society of Alexandria:

The patriot who feels himself in the service of God, who acknowledges Him in all his ways, has the promise of Almighty direction, and will find His Word in his greatest darkness, "a lantern to his feet and a lamp unto his paths"...

He will therefore seek to establish for his country in the eyes of the world, such a character as shall make her not unworthy of the name of a Christian nation.

19.
IN GOD WE TRUST

The 4th verse of "The Star-Spangled Banner" inspired Congress, March 3, 1865, to place the motto "IN GOD WE TRUST" on the nation's coins, as House Speaker Schuyler Colfax noted:

> The last act of Congress ever signed by President Lincoln was one requiring that the motto...'IN GOD WE TRUST' should hereafter be inscribed upon all our national coin.

The motto, "IN GOD WE TRUST," was inscribed in the U.S. House Chamber above the Speaker's rostrum; above the Senate's main southern door; on a tribute block inside the Washington Monument; and on a stained-glass window in the U.S. Capitol's Chapel.

On MARCH 3, 1931, Congress adopted Francis Scott Key's "The Star-Spangled Banner," as the National Anthem.

President Truman stated October 30, 1949:

> When the U.S. was established...the motto was 'IN GOD WE TRUST.' That is still our motto and we still place our firm trust in God.

President Eisenhower remarked at a ceremony issuing the first stamp bearing the motto "IN GOD WE TRUST," April 8, 1954:

> America's greatness has been based upon a spiritual quality...symbolized by the stamp that will be issued today...Regardless of any eloquence of the words that may be inside the letter, on the outside he places a message:
> "Here is...the land that lives in respect for the Almighty's mercy to us."...Each of us, hereafter, fastening such a stamp on a letter, cannot fail to feel something of the inspiration that we do whenever we...read "IN GOD WE TRUST."

The same day, President Eisenhower stated to a Women's Conference:

> I have just come from assisting in the dedication of a new stamp...The stamp has on it a picture of the Statue of Liberty, and on it also is stated "IN GOD WE TRUST"...All of us mere mortals are dependent upon the

mercy of a Superior Being...The reason this seems so thrilling is...the opportunity it gives to every single individual who buys the stamp to send a message—regardless of the content of a letter...that this is the land of the free and "IN GOD WE TRUST."

President Eisenhower stated while marking the 75th Anniversary of the Incandescent Lamp, October 24, 1954:

"IN GOD WE TRUST." Often have we heard the words of this wonderful American motto. Let us make sure that familiarity has not made

them meaningless for us. We carry the torch of freedom as a sacred trust for all mankind. We do not believe that God intended the light that He created to be put out by men.

Eisenhower continued:

Atheism substitutes men for the Supreme Creator and this leads inevitably to domination and dictatorship. But we believe — and it is because we believe that God intends all men to be free and equal that we demand free government. Our Government is servant, not master, our chosen representatives are our equals, not our czars or commissars.

We must jealously guard our foundation in faith. For on it rests the ability of the American individual to live and thrive in this blessed land - and to be able to help other less fortunate people to achieve freedom and individual opportunity. These we take for granted, but to others they are often only a wistful dream.

On July 11, 1954, a month after the phrase "under God" was incorporated into the Pledge of Allegiance, Congress enacted Public Law 84-140 which put the motto, 'IN GOD WE TRUST,' on all national coins and currency.

In 1956, the phrase "IN GOD WE TRUST" was legally adopted by Congress as the United States' National Motto.

John F. Kennedy stated February 9, 1961:

The guiding principle of this Nation has been, is now, and ever shall be "IN GOD WE TRUST."

President Reagan stated in his National Day of Prayer Proclamation, March 19, 1981:

Our Nation's motto 'IN GOD WE TRUST'—was not chosen lightly. It reflects a basic recognition that there is a divine authority in the universe to which this Nation owes homage.

Reagan stated at a White House observance of National Day of Prayer, May 6, 1982:

Our faith in God is a mighty source of strength. Our Pledge of Allegiance states that we are 'one nation under God,' and our currency bears the motto, "IN GOD WE TRUST."

Reagan said following a meeting with Pope John Paul II in Vatican City, June 7, 1982:

Ours is a nation grounded on faith, faith in

man's ability through God-given freedom to live in tolerance and peace and faith that a Supreme Being guides our daily striving in this world. Our national motto, "IN GOD WE TRUST," reflects that faith.

President George H.W. Bush met with Amish and Mennonites at Penn Johns Elementary School in Lancaster, PA, March 22, 1989. When a Mennonite leader stated: "We want to keep that theme, 'IN GOD WE TRUST,' which is stamped on our money," President Bush replied:

It's staying there. Nobody can knock that off.

President George H.W. Bush remarked on the National Day of Prayer, May 4, 1989:

We are one nation under God. And we were placed here on Earth to do His work. And our work has gone on now for more than 200 years in the Nation—a work best embodied in four simple words: "IN GOD WE TRUST."

In a 2003 joint poll, *USA Today*, CNN, and Gallup reported that 90% of Americans support "IN GOD WE TRUST" being on U.S. coins.

In 2006, on the 50th anniversary of its adoption, the Senate reaffirmed "IN GOD WE TRUST" as the official national motto.

In July 2010, a Federal Appeals Court in the District of Columbia ruled 3-0 in favor the National Motto's constitutionality under the First Amendment, quoting the 1970 decision, *Aronow v. United States:*

> It is quite obvious that the national motto and slogan on coinage and currency "IN GOD WE TRUST" has nothing whatsoever to do with the establishment of religion.

In 2011, the House of Representatives passed an additional resolution reaffirming "IN GOD WE TRUST" as the official motto of the United States in a 396-9 vote.

On March 7, 2011, the Supreme Court denied the challenge by an atheist who was intolerant of the National Motto by letting the decision of a Federal Appeals Court stand.

20.
HAND OF PROVIDENCE SHIELDS
AMERICANS FROM BOMBS AND ROCKETS

Though the War of 1812 was effectively over two weeks earlier with the signing of the Treaty of Ghent, December 24, 1814, news had not yet reached New Orleans.

On January 8, 1815, in the last battle of the War of 1812, nearly 10,000 British soldiers advanced under cover of darkness and heavy fog, intending to surprise General Andrew Jackson's Tennessee and Kentucky sharpshooters, aided by French pirate Jean Lafitte and his men. As the British neared, the fog suddenly lifted and in just a half hour 2,042 British were killed or wounded, while there were only 71 American casualties.

General Andrew Jackson wrote on January 26, 1815, to Robert Hays regarding the victorious Battle of New Orleans:

> It appears that the unerring hand of Providence shielded my men from the shower of balls, bombs, and rockets, when every ball and bomb from our guns carried with them a mission of death.

General Jackson told his aide-de-camp Major Davezac of his confidence before the Battle:

> I was sure of success, for I knew that God would not give me previsions of disaster, but signs of victory. He said this ditch can never be passed. It cannot be done.

Andrew Jackson wrote to Secretary of War James Monroe, February 17, 1815:

> Heaven, to be sure, has interposed most wonderfully in our behalf, and I am filled with gratitude, when I look back to what we have escaped.

The Treaty of Ghent was ratified by the U.S. Senate, February 16, 1815. Ten days later, Napoleon escaped from the Island of Elba and all British troops had to be immediately returned to Europe. For the next one hundred days, events in Europe cascaded toward the massive Battle of Waterloo. President Madison proclaimed for the United States a National Day of Thanksgiving to Almighty God, March 4, 1815:

"No people ought to feel greater obligations to celebrate the goodness of the Great Disposer of Events...distinguished by multiplied tokens of His benign interposition."

21.
DAVY CROCKETT DISARMS ASSAILANT TRYING TO KILL ANDREW JACKSON

Alexander Hamilton helped create the Bank of the United States in 1791. By 1822, it

GENERAL JACKSON SLAYING THE MANY HEADED MONSTER.

was run by Nicholas Biddle, who boasted of having more power than the President, as he set interest rates and reserve requirements, owned newspapers, bought influence, and paid to elect politicians.

Andrew Jackson withdrew the Federal funds out of the Bank of the United States and vetoed the renewal of its charter, stating in 1832:

Controlling our currency, receiving our public moneys, and

holding thousands of our citizens in dependence, it would be more... dangerous than the naval and military power of the enemy.

On January 30, 1835, in the midst of the "war with the Bank of the United States," President Andrew Jackson survived an assassination attempt when a bearded man, Richard Lawrence, fired two pistols at him at point blank range.

For some reason the guns misfired.

Davy Crockett, who was with the President, wrestled the assailant down and disarmed him.

When King William IV of England heard of the incident, he wrote expressing his concern. President Jackson wrote back:

A kind of Providence had been pleased to shield me against the recent attempt upon my life, and irresistibly carried many minds to the belief in a superintending Providence.

Andrew Jackson stated in his 2nd Inaugural:

It is my fervent prayer to that Almighty Being before whom I now stand, and who has kept us in His hands from the infancy of our Republic to the present day... that He will...inspire the hearts of my fellow-citizens that we may be preserved from danger.

Andrew Jackson, known as "Old Hickory," wrote in a letter, March 25, 1835:

I was brought up a rigid Presbyterian, to which I have always adhered. Our excellent Constitution guarantees to every one freedom of religion, and charity tells us - and you know charity is the real basis of all true religion - ...judge the tree by its fruit.

All who profess Christianity believe in a Saviour, and that by and through Him we must be saved...We ought, therefore, to consider all good Christians whose walks correspond with their professions, be they Presbyterian, Episcopalian, Baptist, Methodist or Roman Catholic.

Jackson carried a bullet in his body from a duel defending the honor of his wife, Rachel. She died three months before he took office as the 7th President, resulting in his niece, Emily Donelson, filling the role of the First Lady. When Emily died, Andrew Jackson wrote to her husband, Col. A.J. Donelson, December 30, 1836:

We cannot recall her, we are commanded by our dear Saviour, not to mourn for the dead, but for the living...She has changed a world of woe for a world of eternal happiness, and we ought to prepare as we too must follow..."The Lord's will be done on earth as it is in heaven."

Of the Bible, Andrew Jackson stated: "That book, Sir, is the Rock upon which our Republic rests."

22.
CHOLERA EPIDEMIC DEATHS DROP SUDDENLY AFTER PRAYER

In India, a religious practice for some people was to bathe in the sewage-filled Ganges River. As a result, they would contract a waterborne disease called cholera.

The British Empire was the largest empire in world history, controlling over 13 million square miles and ruling over a half billion people. When the British East India Company gained control of India in the early 1800's, they built railroads and sent steamboats up the rivers. Unfortunately, individuals infected with cholera were able to quickly travel back to Europe, carrying the disease with them.

It killed tens of millions in crowded cities in England, Ireland, Belgium, Netherlands, France, Spain, Italy, Germany, Hungary, China, Japan, Java, Korea, the Philippines, India, Bengal, Iran, Iraq, Algeria, Tunisia, Egypt, Arabia, and Africa. In Russia alone, cholera killed over one million people. Even the famous composer, Tchaikovsky, died from cholera.

Spreading through unsanitary water, infected immigrants carried cholera to America, Canada, Mexico, Venezuela, Brazil, and the Pacific Coast.

In 1832, as the Asiatic cholera outbreak gripped New York, Henry Clay asked for a Joint Resolution of Congress to request the President set:

> A Day of Public Humiliation, Prayer and Fasting to be observed by the people of the United States with religious solemnity.

By 1849, cholera killed 5,000 in New York, (a mass grave was dug on Randall's Island in the East River); 8,000 were killed in Cincinnati; and 3,000 were killed in New Orleans. It spread up the Mississippi and 5,000 were killed in St. Louis (6% of the city's population), including Pierre Chouteau, Sr., one of St. Louis' prominent early settlers.

In Chicago, 3,500 died. Harriett Beecher Stowe's infant son died, as well as former 11th U.S. President James K. Polk. Ohio had to postpone its first Ohio State Fair. Cholera spread along the Oregon Trail

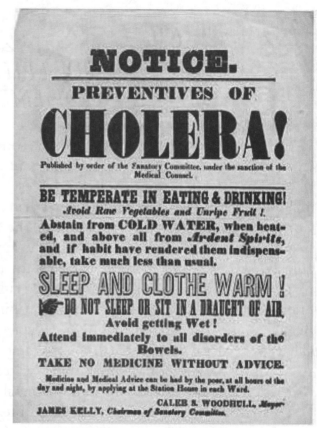

to the Pacific Northwest and the Mormon Trail to Utah. It killed an estimated 12,000 on their way to the California Gold Rush. In total, an estimated 150,000 Americans died from cholera.

The President at the time was General Zachary Taylor, known as "Old Rough and Ready" for fighting the British in the War of 1812, the Sac Indians in the Black Hawk War and the Seminole Indians in Florida. Taylor's victories in the Mexican War, in the face of being greatly outnumbered by Santa Anna's forces, made him a national hero.

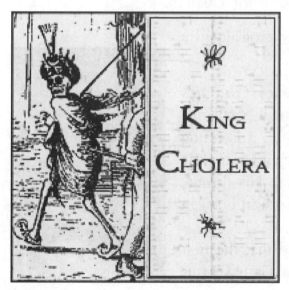

Elected the 12th U.S. President, Zachary Taylor refused to be sworn in on the Sabbath out of respect. President Zachary Taylor was presented with a Bible by a delegation of ladies from Frankfort, Kentucky. His acknowledgment was printed in the *Frankfort Commonwealth*, February 21, 1849:

I accept with gratitude...your gift of this inestimable Volume. It was for the love of the truths of this great Book that our fathers abandoned their native shores for the wilderness. Animated by its lofty principles they toiled and suffered till the desert blossomed as a rose.

The same truths sustained them...to become a free nation; and guided by the wisdom of this Book they founded a government.

On July 4, 1849, President Taylor told a Sabbath-School celebration in Washington:

The only ground of hope for the continuance of our free institutions is in the proper moral and religious training of the children.

On July 3, 1849, President Zachary Taylor proclaimed a National Day of Fasting:

At a season when the providence of God has manifested itself in the visitation of a fearful pestilence which is spreading itself throughout the land, it is fitting that a people whose reliance has ever been in His protection should humble themselves before His throne, and, while acknowledging past transgressions, ask a continuance of the Divine mercy.

It is therefore earnestly recommended that the first Friday in August be observed throughout the United States as a Day of Fasting, Humiliation, and Prayer...

It is recommended to persons of all religious denominations to abstain as far as practical from secular occupations and to assemble in their respective places of public worship, to acknowledge the Infinite Goodness which has watched over our existence as a nation, and so long crowned us with manifold blessings, and to implore the Almighty in His own good time to stay the destroying hand which is now lifted up against us.

New Jersey Governor Daniel Haines's proclamation was published in the *Paterson Intelligencer,* August 1, 1849:

Whereas the President of the United States, in consideration of the prevailing pestilence, has set...a Day of Fasting...

and whereas I believe that the people of this State recognize the obligations of a Christian nation publicly to acknowledge their dependence upon Almighty God...

that abstaining from their worldly pursuits, they assemble...with humble confession of sin...and fervently...

implore the Almighty Ruler of the Universe, to remove us from the scourge...and speedily...restore to us the inestimable blessing of health.

Mayor John Howard of Dayton, Ohio, proclaimed a Day of Fasting and ordered all stores to be closed. Hundreds of people knelt openly in the streets and prayed.

Tim O'Neil wrote "A Look Back: Cholera Epidemic Hit a Peak Here in 1849" (STLToday.com):

Cholera first reached St. Louis from Europe in 1832, killing 300, and returned in each of the next three summers...St. Louis was a fast-growing city of 75,000, with immigrants arriving by the steamboat-load. It also had no sewer system...More than 120 died of cholera in April 1849...The toll grew six-fold in May...reached 2,200 in July...in late July with a weekly toll of 640, seven times the city's normal death rate...

The worst death rates were in the slums on the north and south ends of present-day downtown, where bodies were buried in ditches...

Cholera also killed Pierre Chouteau, Sr., a member of the founding family...Cholera killed at least 6 percent of the city's population...The official death toll was 4,317...

The number of deaths dropped suddenly in August.

CHOLERA AT MERTHYR-TYDFIL. RETURN OF CASES, Saturday, September 22, 1849.	ATTACKED	DEAD
MERTHYR. Total from commencement (May 25th), as per last Report, corrected by Registration Returns up to 10 A.M., Yesterday	1779	745
New Cases, up to 10 A.M., To-day	1	1
PENYDARRAN. Total from commencement (June 5th), up to 10 A.M., Yesterday	272	170
New Cases, up to 10 A.M., To-day	0	0
DOWLAIS. Total from commencement (June 10th), up to 10 A.M., Yesterday	1196	499
New Cases, up to 10 A.M., To-day	0	1
ABERDARE. Total from commencement (June 24th), up to 10 A.M., Yesterday	364	104
New Cases, up to 10 A.M., To-day	0	0
TOTAL	3612	1520

FRANK JAMES,
Clerk to the Guardians.

President Taylor's Proclamation of Fasting was observed August 3, 1849, and by the end of the month, the death toll had "dropped suddenly."

23.
FREAK ACCIDENT CHANGES COURSE
OF CIVIL WAR DAYS AFTER PRAYER

On December 14, 1860, President James Buchanan issued a Proclamation of a National Day of Humiliation, Fasting and Prayer:

> In this the hour of our calamity and peril to whom shall we resort for relief but to the God of our fathers? His omnipotent arm only can save us from the awful effects of our own crimes and follies...
> Let us...unite in humbling ourselves before the Most High, in confessing our individual and national sins...Let me invoke every individual, in whatever sphere of life he may be placed, to feel a personal responsibility to God and his country for keeping this day holy.

On August 12, 1861, after the Union lost the Battle of Bull Run, President Abraham Lincoln proclaimed:

It is fit...to acknowledge and revere the Supreme Government of God; to bow in humble submission to His chastisement; to confess and deplore their sins and transgressions in the full conviction that the fear of the Lord is the beginning of wisdom...

Therefore I, Abraham Lincoln...do appoint the last Thursday in September next as a Day of Humiliation, Prayer and Fasting for all the people of the nation.

Later, President Lincoln proclaimed a National Day of Humiliation, Fasting and Prayer, March 30, 1863:

Whereas, the Senate of the United States devoutly recognizing the Supreme Authority and just Government of Almighty God in all the affairs of men and of nations, has, by a resolution, requested the President to designate and set apart a day for national prayer and humiliation; and

Whereas, it is the duty of nations as well as of men to own their dependence upon the overruling power of God, to confess their sins and transgressions in humble sorrow yet with assured hope that genuine repentance will lead to mercy and pardon, and to recognize the sublime truth, announced in the Holy Scriptures and proven by all history: that those nations only are blessed whose God is the Lord;

And, insomuch as we know that, by His divine law, nations like individuals are subjected to punishments and chastisement in this world, may we not justly fear that the awful calamity of civil war, which now desolates the land may be but a punishment inflicted upon us for our presumptuous sins to the needful end of our national reformation as a whole people?

We have been the recipients of the choicest bounties of Heaven. We have been preserved these many years in peace and prosperity. We have grown in numbers, wealth and power as no other nation has ever grown.

But we have forgotten God. We have forgotten the gracious Hand which preserved us in peace, and multiplied and enriched and strengthened us; and we have vainly imagined, in the deceitfulness of our hearts, that all these blessings were produced by some superior wisdom and virtue of our own.

Intoxicated with unbroken success, we have become too self-sufficient to feel the necessity of redeeming and preserving grace, too proud to pray to the God that made us!

It behooves us then to humble ourselves before the offended Power, to confess our national sins and to pray for clemency and forgiveness.

Now, therefore, in compliance with the request and fully concurring in the view of the Senate, I do, by this my proclamation, designate and set apart Thursday, the 30th day of April, 1863, as a day of national humiliation, fasting and prayer.

And I do hereby request all the people to abstain on that day from their ordinary secular pursuits, and to unite, at their several places of public worship and their respective homes, in keeping the day holy to the Lord and devoted to the humble discharge of the religious duties proper to that solemn occasion.

All this being done, in sincerity and truth, let us then rest humbly in the hope authorized by the Divine teachings, that the united cry of the nation will be heard on high and answered with blessing no less than the pardon of our national sins and the restoration of our now divided and suffering country to its former happy condition of unity and peace.

In witness whereof, I have hereunto set my hand and caused the seal of the United States to be affixed.

Lincoln's National Day of Humiliation, Fasting & Prayer was observed April 30, 1863. Two days later, a freak accident changed the course of the war.

Lt. General Thomas J. "Stonewall" Jackson was considered one of the greatest tactical commanders in history. He refused to let his men give ground at the First Battle of Bull Run (July 21, 1861), standing there "like a stonewall."

Often outnumbered 7 to 3, Jackson successfully fought the Shenandoah Valley Campaign: Battles of McDowell (May 8, 1862), Front Royal (May 23, 1862), Winchester (May 25, 1862), and Port Republic (June 9, 1862); and Seven Days Battles (June 25-July 1, 1862), Second Battle of Bull Run (August 28-30, 1862), Antietam (September 17, 1862), Fredericksburg (December 11-15, 1862) and Chancellorsville (April 30-May 2, 1863).

On May 2, 1863, after successfully attacking the Union flank in the Battle of Chancellorville, Jackson surveyed the field and returned to camp at twilight.

Suddenly, one of his own men shouted, "Halt, who goes there," and without waiting for a reply, a volley of shots were fired. Two bullets hit General Jackson's left arm and one hit his right hand. Several men accompanying him were killed, in addition to many horses. In the confusion that followed, Jackson was dropped from his stretcher while being evacuated. His left arm had to be amputated. General Robert E. Lee wrote to Jackson:

> Could I have directed events, I would have chosen for the good of the country to be disabled in your stead.

General Lee sent the message through Chaplain B.T. Lacy:

> He has lost his left arm but I my right...
> Tell him that I wrestled in prayer for him last night...as I never prayed for myself.

Growing weaker with a pneumonia, Jackson said, May 10, 1863:

It is the Lord's Day; my wish is fulfilled. I have always desired to die on Sunday.

A few moments before he died, as he was losing consciousness, he said:

Let us cross over the river, and rest under the shade of the trees.

Civil War historians hold the opinion that had General Stonewall Jackson been alive and commanded two months later at the Battle of Gettysburg, the South may have won the battle, and possibly the war.

Jackson's death was difficult to reconcile. Loyal to Virginia, he was exemplary in faith and virtue. He was against slavery and freed the slaves he inherited from his wife's estate. He participated in civil disobedience every Sunday by violating a Virginia law which forbade teaching slaves to read. Beginning in 1855, Jackson financed and taught a Colored Sunday School class at the Lexington Presbyterian Church where he taught slaves and free blacks, both adults and children, to read the Bible.

President Franklin D. Roosevelt stated, September 17, 1937:

I came into the world 17 years after the close of the war between the States...Today...there are still many among us who can remember it...It serves us little to discuss again the rights and the wrongs of the long 4-years' war...

We can but wish that the war had never been. We can and we do revere the memory of the brave men who fought on both sides...

But we know today that it was best...for the generations of Americans who have come after them, that the conflict did not end in a division of our land into two nations. I like to think that it was the will of God that we remain one people.

At the Confederate Memorial in Arlington Cemetery, President Coolidge said, May 25, 1924:

It was Lincoln who pointed out that both sides prayed to the same God. When that is the case, it is only a matter of time when each will seek a common end. We can now see clearly what that end is. It is the maintenance of our American ideals, beneath a common flag, under the blessings of Almighty God.

24.
CLARA BARTON BEGINS AMERICAN RED CROSS

Clara Barton was a schoolteacher who moved to Washington at the outbreak of the Civil War. The first woman to be a clerk at the U.S. Patent Office, Clara Barton volunteered to distribute relief supplies to wounded soldiers and, at the request of President Lincoln, aided for nearly four years in searching for missing soldiers.

After attempting to carry a wounded soldier off the battlefield of Antietam, September 17, 1862, Clara Barton said:

> A ball had passed between my body and the right arm which supported him, cutting through the sleeve and passing through his chest from shoulder to shoulder. There was no more to be done for him and I left him to his rest. I have never mended that hole in my sleeve. I wonder if a soldier ever does mend a bullet hole in his coat?

Clara Barton was present at some of the bloodiest battles of the Civil War: Cedar Mountain, Second Manassas, Antietam, and Fredericksburg.

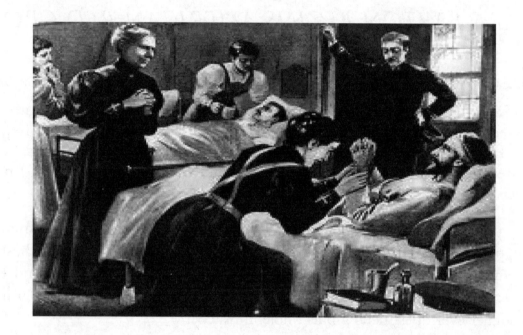

Clara Barton wrote of the soldiers:

> What could I do but go with them, or work for them and my country?
> The patriot blood of my father was warm in my veins.

The National Park Service recorded that Clara Barton first visited Chatham or "Lacy House" in early August 1862, bringing food and hospital supplies to help "her boys." She returned during the Fredericksburg Campaign, December 1862.

Clara Barton helped care for the wounded soldiers of both sides that were brought into the house. A physician requested her help in the city, which required her to cross a pontoon bridge over the river. As she stepped off, an officer offered her his hand. Suddenly a shell passed under their arms, tearing away part of her skirt and his coattail. He later died.

Clara Barton set up a soup kitchen at the Lacy House, which became a makeshift hospital for the Union 2nd Corps. With doctors too busy to keep medical records, Clara wrote in her diary the names of the men who died and where they were buried. Her diary is at the Clara Barton National Historic Site in Maryland.

On December 13, the day of the heaviest fighting, Clara was in the doorway of the Lacy House when an exploding shell severed a soldier's artery. She applied the tourniquet that saved his life. Crossing the river again, a Union provost marshall thought she was a civilian and volunteered to escort her to safety, but looking at the thousands of Union

soldiers, she politely declined the offer saying she was the best protected woman in the world. When a shell struck the door of the room she was in, "she did not flinch, but continued her duties" assisting the doctors.

The next two weeks at Chatham, Clara saw "hundreds of the worst wounded men I have ever seen," occupying every room of the house. They "covered every foot of the floors and porticos" and stair landings. A man "thought himself rich" if he laid under a table where he would not be stepped on. Clara saw five men stuffed onto four shelves of a cupboard. Others shivered in the cold muddy yard on blankets, waiting for someone inside to die so they could be brought in.

Clara set up a soup kitchen in a tent in the yard to help them. The Library of Congress has the letter Clara Barton wrote to her cousin:

> Head Quarters 2nd Div.
> 9th Army Corps-Army of the Potomac
> Camp near Falmouth, Va.
> December 12th, 1862 - 2 o'clock A.M.
> My dear Cousin Vira:
> Five minutes time with you; and God only knows what those five
> minutes might be worth to the many-doomed thousands sleeping around me.
> It is the night before a battle. The enemy, Fredericksburg, and its

mighty entrenchments lie before us, the river between - at tomorrow's dawn our troops will assay to cross, and the guns of the enemy will sweep those frail bridges at every breath.

The moon is shining through the soft haze with a brightness almost prophetic. For the last half hour I have stood alone in the awful stillness of its glimmering light gazing upon the strange sad scene around me striving to say, "Thy will Oh God be done."

The camp fires blaze with unwanted brightness, the sentry's tread is still but quick - the acres of little shelter tents are dark and still as death, no wonder for us as I gazed sorrowfully upon them.

I thought I could almost hear the slow flap of the grim messenger's wings, as one by one he sought and selected his victims for the morning sacrifice.

Sleep weary one, sleep and rest for tomorrow's toil. Oh! Sleep and visit in dreams once more the loved ones nestling at home. They may yet live to dream of you, cold lifeless and bloody, but this dream, soldier, is thy last, paint it brightly, dream it well.

Oh northern mothers, wives and sisters, all unconscious of the hour, would to Heaven that I could bear for you the concentrated woe which is so soon to follow, would that Christ would teach my soul a prayer that would plead to the Father for grace sufficient for you. God pity and strengthen you every one.

Mine are not the only waking hours, the light yet burns brightly in our kind hearted General's tent where he pens what may be a last farewell to his wife and children and thinks sadly of his fated men. Already the roll of the moving artillery is sounded in my ears.

The battle draws near and I must catch one hour's sleep for tomorrow's labor. Good night, dear cousin, and Heaven grant you strength for your more peaceful and less terrible, but not less weary days than mine. Yours in love, Clara.

Later Clara Barton stated:

In time of peace we must prepare for war, and it is no less a wise benevolence that makes preparation in the hour of peace for assuaging the ills that are sure to accompany war...

I have an almost complete disregard of precedent, and a faith in the possibility of something better...I cannot afford the luxury of a closed mind. I go for anything new that might improve the past.

Clara Barton then went to Europe during the Franco-German War, where she worked with Henri Dunant, founder of the International Red Cross. Henri Dunant was the first recipient of the Nobel Peace Prize. He founded the Geneva chapter of the Young Men's Christian Association (YMCA) and proposed Jews repopulate Palestine, being one of the few non-Jews to attend the First Zionist Congress in Basel, 1897. Theodore Herzl first used the term, "Christian Zionist" in reference to him.

Inspired by Henri Dunant's International Red Cross, Clara Barton established the American Red Cross Society, May 21, 1881, serving as its head until 1904. Clara Barton stated:

An institution or reform movement that is not selfish, must originate in the recognition of some evil that is adding to the sum of human suffering, or diminishing the sum of happiness. I may be compelled to face danger, but never fear it, and while our soldiers can stand and fight, I can stand and feed and nurse them.

I am well and strong and young - young enough to go to the front. If I cannot be a soldier, I'll help soldiers.

Clara Barton helped in hospitals in Cuba during the Spanish-American War. President William McKinley spoke of Clara Barton in his Message, December 5, 1898:

It is a pleasure for me to mention in terms of cordial appreciation the timely and useful work of the American National Red Cross, both in relief measures preparatory to the campaigns, in sanitary assistance at several of

the camps of assemblage, and later, under the able and experienced leadership of the president of the society, **Miss Clara Barton**, on the fields of battle and in the hospitals at the front in Cuba.

Working in conjunction with the governmental authorities and under their sanction and approval, and with the enthusiastic cooperation of many patriotic women and societies in the various States, **the Red Cross** has fully maintained its already high reputation for intense earnestness and ability to exercise the noble purposes of its international organization, thus justifying the confidence and support which it has received at the hands of the American people.

To the members and officers of this society and all who aided them in their philanthropic work the sincere and lasting gratitude of the soldiers and the public is due and is freely accorded.

In tracing these events we are constantly reminded of our obligations to the Divine Master for His watchful care over us and His safe guidance, for which the nation makes reverent acknowledgment and offers humble prayer for the continuance of His favor.

President Woodrow Wilson mentioned the Red Cross in his Proclamation of a Contribution Day for the aid of stricken Jewish people, January 11, 1916:

Whereas in the various countries now engaged in war there are nine millions of Jews, the great majority of whom are destitute of food, shelter, and clothing; and...have been driven from their homes without warning, deprived of an opportunity to make provision for their most elementary wants, causing starvation, disease and untold suffering; and

Whereas the people of the United States of America have learned with sorrow of this terrible plight of millions of human beings and have most generously responded to the cry for help...

I, Woodrow Wilson, President of the United States...appoint...January 27, 1916, as a day upon which the people of the United States may make such contributions...for the aid of the stricken Jewish people. Contributions may be addressed to the American Red Cross, Washington, D.C.

At the Second Red Cross Drive in New York City, President Wilson stated, May 18, 1918:

Being members of the American Red Cross...a great fraternity and fellowship which extends all over the world...this cross which these ladies bore here today is an emblem of Christianity itself...

When you think of this, you realize how the people of the United States are being drawn together into a great intimate family whose heart is being used for the service of the soldiers not only, but for the long night of suffering and terror, in order that they and men everywhere may see the dawn of a day of righteousness and justice and peace.

On December 8, 1918, in an appeal of support for the American Red Cross just a month after the fighting in World War I had ceased, President Woodrow Wilson stated:

One year ago, 22 million Americans, by enrolling as members of the Red Cross at Christmas time, sent to the men who were fighting our battles overseas a stimulating message of cheer and good-will...Now, by God's grace, the Red Cross Christmas message of 1918 is to be a message of peace as well as a message of good-will.

On May 1, 1940, President Franklin D. Roosevelt greeted the chairman of the American National Red Cross, Norman H. Davis, in Washington, D.C.:

The great International Red Cross organization, founded 76 years ago to bring mercy to the battlefield...I am confident that whatever may be the problems which intensification of warfare may bring, the American people will respond to any appeal for funds when the Red Cross deems it necessary to call upon them for additional aid. By such response we can aid in sustaining the spirit and morale of those in distress abroad until the happy day we all pray for, when hostilities shall cease.

25.
WORLD WAR I TURNS TO VICTORY FOR ALLIES

During World War I, there was an unofficial "Christmas Truce" during the winter of 1914. The song "Silent Night" was sung across the battle lines by German, French, and English troops, as it was one of the few carols that soldiers on both sides knew. They ventured out of their trenches and spent the day visiting, playing soccer, trading souvenirs and sharing food. Afterwards, irate commanders on both sides forbade unauthorized fraternizing with the enemy.

After the sinking of the *Lusitania* by Kaiser Wilhelm's Germany U-boats in 1915, public opinion in America changed. The United States entered World War I on April 6, 1917. Soon, Americans were arriving at the rate of 10,000 a day to fight "the Hun." George M. Cohen wrote the popular song, "Over There," for which he was awarded a Congressional Gold Medal by President Roosevelt in 1936:

> Over there, over there,
> Send the word, send the word over there
> That the Yanks are coming, the Yanks are coming

The drums rum-tumming everywhere.
So prepare, say a prayer,
Send the word, send the word to beware -
We'll be over, we're coming over,
And we won't come back till it's over, over there.

Within two years, America enlisted 4 million soldiers and spent 35 billion dollars. Soldiers were given New Testaments and Book of Psalms containing Prefaces written by President Woodrow Wilson, former President Theodore Roosevelt and General John J. Pershing, who wrote:

Hardship will be your lot, but trust in God will give you comfort; temptation will befall you, but the teachings of our Savior will give you strength.

Germany's Red Baron dominated the skies. An American pilot shot down was Quentin Roosevelt, son of the former President. A race car driver, Eddie Rickenbacker, transferred from being General Pershing's chauffeur to flying in the 94th Aero Pursuit Squandron, which shot down 69 enemy aricraft. Escaping death many times, Eddie Rickenbacker wrote:

I am not such an egotist as to believe that God has spared me because I am I.

I believe there is work for me to do and that I am spared to do it, just as you are.

President Wilson stated April 16, 1917:

This is the time for America... I hope that the clergymen will not think the theme of it an unworthy or inappropriate subject of comment and homily from their pulpits.

President Wilson told the Grand Army of the Republic, May 30, 1917:

In the providence of God, America will once more have an opportunity to show the world that she was born to serve mankind.

Pope Benedict XV, August 1, 1917, offered to mediate peace between European Powers:

Do not...turn a deaf ear to our prayer, accept the...invitation which we extend to you in the name of the Divine Redeemer, Prince of Peace.

Bear in mind your very grave responsibility to God and man; on your decision depend...the lives of thousands of young men.

On September 3, 1917, President Woodrow Wilson wrote to the National Army:

My affectionate confidence goes with you in every battle and every test. God keep and guide you!

President Wilson proclaimed a Day of Prayer, October 19, 1917:

Congress, in view of the entrance of our nation into the vast and awful war...has requested me to set apart...a day upon which our people should be called upon to offer concerted prayer to Almighty God for His divine aid in the success of our arms...

It behooves...a nation which has sought from the earliest days of its

existence to be obedient to the divine teachings which have inspired it in the exercise of its liberties, to turn always to the Supreme Master and cast themselves in faith at His feet.

On December 4, 1917, President Woodrow Wilson addressed Congress:

A supreme moment of history has come...The hand of God is laid upon the nations. He will show them favor, I devoutly believe, only if they rise to the clear heights of His own justice and mercy.

President Wilson gave an Executive Order to the Army and Navy, January 20, 1918:

The President, commander in chief of the Army and Navy...enjoins the orderly observance of the Sabbath by the officers and men in the military and naval service of the United States.

The importance for man and beast of the prescribed weekly rest, the sacred rights of Christian soldiers and sailors, a becoming deference to the best sentiment of a Christian people, and a due regard for the Divine Will demand that Sunday labor in the Army and Navy be reduced to the measure of strict necessity.

On May 11, 1918, President Wilson proclaimed

It being the duty peculiarly incumbent in a time of war...to acknowledge our dependence on Almighty God and to implore His aid and protection...a Day of Public Humiliation, Prayer and Fasting...be observed by the people of the United States with religious solemnity and the offering of fervent supplications to Almighty God for the safety and welfare of our cause, His blessings on our arms, and a speedy restoration of an honorable and lasting peace to the nations of the earth...

Therefore, I...exhort my fellow-citizens of all faiths and creeds to assemble on that day in their several places of worship and there...to pray Almighty God that He may forgive our sins.

Less than a month later, May 28, 1918, four U.S. divisions were deployed with French and British troops and they won the Battle of Cantigny, America's first offensive of the war.

On October 8, 1918, an American battalion was pinned down by machine gun fire along the Decauville rail-line north of Chatel-Chehery, France.

Sergeant Alvin. C. York described:

The Germans got us...They stopped us dead in our tracks. Their machine guns were up there on the heights overlooking us and well hidden, and we couldn't tell for certain where the terrible heavy fire was coming from...Those machine guns were spitting fire and cutting down the undergrowth all around me.

With all but 8 killed, Sergeant York took charge and proceeded to take out 32 machine guns, kill 28 of the enemy and captured 132. He received the Medal of Honor, stating:

Some of them officers have been saying that I being a mountain boy and accustomed to the woods...done all these things the right way jes by instinct...I hadn't never got much larnin' from books, except the Bible. Maybe my instincts are more natural...but that ain't enough to account for the way I come out alive, with all those German soldiers raining death on me...

I'm a-telling you the hand of God must have been in that fight... Jes think of them 30 machine guns raining fire on me point-blank from a range of only 25 yards and all them-there rifles and pistols besides, those bombs, and then those men charged with fixed bayonets, and I never receiving a scratch, and bringing 132 prisoners. I have got only one explanation...that God must have heard my prayers.

The war ended with the signing of the Armistice, November 11, 1918. Five days later, President Wilson proclaimed:

> Complete victory has brought us... God has indeed been gracious...While we render thanks...let us not forget to seek the Divine guidance...and divine mercy and forgiveness... Wherefore, I...designate...a Day of Thanksgiving and Prayer...to render thanks to God, the Ruler of Nations.

President Wilson said in his 6th Annual Address, December 2, 1918:

> What we all thank God for with deepest gratitude is that our men went in force into the line of battle just at the critical moment when the whole fate of the world seemed to hang in the balance.

26.
GEORGE WASHINGTON CARVER'S ANSWERED PRAYERS SAVE SOUTHERN ECONOMY

George Washington Carver was born a slave during the Civil War, possibly in 1865, but there are no records. Within a few weeks, his father, who belonged to the next farm over, was killed in a log hauling accident. Shortly after the Civil War, while still an infant, George, with his mother and sister, was kidnapped by bushwhackers.

Moses Carver sent friends to track down the thieves and trade his best horse to retrieve them. The thieves only left baby George, lying on the ground, sick with the whooping cough. George never saw his mother and sister again. Illness claimed the lives of his two other sisters and they were buried on the Carver farm. George and his older brother, Jim, were raised in Diamond Grove, Missouri, by "Uncle" Moses and "Aunt" Sue Carver, a childless German immigrant couple.

In poor health as a child, George stayed near the house helping with chores, learning to cook, clean, sew, mend and wash laundry. His recreation was to spend time in the woods.

George worked his way through school and eventually he taught on staff at Iowa State College. In the fall of 1896, George surprised the staff at Iowa State College by announcing his plans to give up his promising future there and join the Tuskegee Institute in Alabama. The staff showed their appreciation by purchasing him a going away present, a microscope, which he used extensively throughout his career.

George assembled an Agricultural Department at Tuskegee. He visited nearby farmers and would teach them farming techniques, such as crop rotation, fertilization and erosion prevention.

Carver noticed that the soil was depleted due to years of repeated cotton growth and

produced very poorly. During this time, an insect called the boll weevil swept through the South, destroying cotton crops and leaving farmers devastated.

George showed the farmers the benefits of crop rotation and planting legumes, such as peanuts, which replenish the soil with nitrogen.

Farmers heeded Carver's advice but soon had more peanuts than the market wanted, as peanuts were primarily used as animal feed. George determined to find more uses for the peanut to increase the market for them. Carver discovered and popularized hundreds of uses for the peanut. He did the same for the sweet potato, pecan, soybean, cowpea, wild plum, and okra.

A partial list of items derived from peanuts was compiled by the Carver Museum at Tuskegee:

BEVERAGES: blackberry punch, cherry punch, lemon punch, orange punch, peanut punch, beverage for ice cream, evaporated peanut beverage; dry coffee, instant coffee, 32 different kinds of milk, dehydrated milk flakes, buttermilk

FOODS: peanut butter, salted peanuts, peanut flour, peanut flakes, peanut meal, cream from peanut milk, butter from peanut milk, egg yolk, breakfast food, bisque powder, cheese, cream cheese, cheese pimento, cheese sandwich, cheese tutti frutti, cocoa, crystallized peanuts, curds, granulated potatoes, potato nibs, golden nuts, mock coconut, pancake flour, peanut hearts, peanut surprise, peanut wafers, pickle, sweet pickle, shredded peanuts, substitute asparagus.

How did George think of making all of these wonderful things from simple farm ingredients? George Carver prayed every time he entered his laboratory which he named "God's Little Workshop." He credited Divine inspiration for giving him ideas regarding how to perform experiments.

In the summer of 1920, the Young Men's Christian Association of Blue Ridge, North Carolina, invited Professor Carver to speak at their summer school for the southern states.

Dr. Willis D. Weatherford, President of Blue Ridge, introduced him as the speaker. With his high voice surprising the audience, Dr. Carver exclaimed humorously:

I always look forward to introductions as opportunities to learn something about myself....

He continued:

Years ago I went into my laboratory and said, "Dear Mr. Creator, please tell me what the universe was made for?"

The Great Creator answered, "You want to know too much for that little mind of yours. Ask for something more your size, little man."

Then I asked, "Please, Mr. Creator, tell me what man was made for."

Again the Great Creator replied, "You are still asking too much. Cut down on the extent and improve the intent."

So then I asked, "Please, Mr. Creator, will you tell me why the peanut was made?"

"That's better, but even then it's infinite. What do you want to know about the peanut?"

"Mr. Creator, can I make milk out of the peanut?"

"What kind of milk do you want? Good Jersey milk or just plain boarding house milk?"

"Good Jersey milk."

And then the Great Creator taught me to take the peanut apart and put it together again. And out of the process have come forth all these products!

Among the numerous products displayed was a bottle of good Jersey milk. Three-and-a-half ounces of peanuts produced one pint of rich milk or one quart of raw "skim" milk, called boarding house "blue john" milk.

On January 21, 1921, at the request of the United Peanut Growers Association, George W. Carver addressed the U.S. House Ways and Means Committee in Washington, D.C., regarding a proposed tariff on imported peanuts. George expounded on the many potential uses of the peanut as a means to improve the Southern economy. Initially given only ten minutes to speak, George Carver so enthralled the committee that the Chairman said,

Go ahead Brother. Your time is unlimited!

George spoke for one hour and forty-five minutes, explaining the many food products derived from the peanut:

If you go to the first chapter of Genesis, we can interpret very clearly, I think, what God intended when he said, "Behold, I have given you every herb that bears seed. To you it shall be meat." This is what He means about it. It shall be meat. There is everything there to strengthen and nourish and keep the body alive and healthy.

The Committee Chairman asked Carver:

"Dr. Carver, how did you learn all of these things?"

Carver answered, "From an old book."

"What book?" asked the Chairman.

Carver replied, "The Bible."

The Chairman inquired, "Does the Bible tell about peanuts?"

"No, Sir" Carver replied, "But it tells about the God who made the peanut. I asked Him to show me what to do with the peanut, and He did."

On November 19, 1924, Carver spoke to over 500 people at the Women's Board of Domestic Missions:

> God is going to reveal to us things He never revealed before if we put our hands in His. No books ever go into my laboratory. The thing I am to do and the way are revealed to me the moment I am inspired to create something new. Without God to draw aside the curtain, I would be helpless.
>
> Only alone can I draw close enough to God to discover His secrets.

On March 24, 1925, Carver wrote to Robert Johnson, an employee of Chesley Enterprises of Ontario:

Thank God I love humanity; complexion doesn't interest me one single bit.

On July 10, 1924, George Washington Carver wrote to James Hardwick:

> God cannot use you as He wishes until you come into the fullness of His Glory. Do not get alarmed, my friend, when doubts creep in. That is old Satan.
>
> Pray, pray, pray. Oh, my friend, I am praying that God will come in and rid you entirely of self so you can go out after souls right, or rather have souls seek the Christ in you.
>
> This is my prayer for you always.

27.
PRAYER FOR GREAT DEPRESSION TO END

October 29, 1929, the New York Stock Exchange crashed. Panic ensued as Wall Street sold 16,410,030 shares in a single day. Billions of dollars were lost and America plunged into the Great Depression.

In a drive to aid private relief agencies, October 18, 1931, President Hoover said:

> Time and again the American people have demonstrated a spiritual quality of generosity...This is the occasion when we must arouse that idealism, that spirit, from which there can be no failure in this primary obligation of every man to his neighbor.

Hoover continued:

> Our country and the world are today involved in more than a financial crisis. We are faced with the primary question of human

MIRACLES IN AMERICAN HISTORY - SUSIE FEDERER

relations, which reaches to the very depths of organized society and to the very depths of human conscience...

This great complex, which we call American life, is builded and can alone survive upon the translation into individual action of that fundamental philosophy announced by the Savior nineteen centuries ago.

Hoover concluded:

Part of our national suffering today is from failure to observe these primary yet inexorable laws of human relationship... Modern society cannot survive with the defense of Cain, "Am I my brother's keeper?"

President Herbert Hoover stated at the Gridiron Club, April 27, 1931:

If, by the grace of God, we have passed the worst of this storm, the future months will be easy. If we shall be called upon to endure more of this period, we must gird ourselves for even greater effort. If we can maintain this courage and resolution we shall have written this new chapter in national life in terms to which our whole idealism has aspired. May God grant to us the spirit and strength to carry through to the end.

Herbert Hoover stated at Valley Forge, May 30, 1931:

If those few thousand men endured that long winter of privation and suffering, humiliated by the despair of their countrymen, and deprived of support save their own indomitable will, yet held their countrymen to the faith, and by that holding held fast the freedom of America, what right have we to be of little faith?

President Herbert Hoover told the National Drive Committee for Voluntary Relief Agencies, September 15, 1932:

Our tasks are definite... that we maintain the spiritual impulses in our people for generous giving and generous service - in the spirit that each

is his brother's keeper...Many a family today is carrying a neighbor family over the trough of this depression not alone with material aid but with that encouragement which maintains courage and faith.

President Herbert Hoover wrote in *The Challenge of Liberty*, 1934:

While I can make no claim for having introduced the term, 'rugged individualism,' I should be proud to have invented it. It has been used by American leaders for over a half-century in eulogy of those God-fearing men and women of honesty whose stamina and character and fearless assertion of rights led them to make their own way in life.

President Herbert Hoover stated in San Diego, California, September 17, 1935:

The American system of liberty...is based upon certain inalienable freedoms and protections which in no event the government may infringe and which we call the Bill of Rights...

They are as clear as the Ten Commandments. Among others the freedom of worship, freedom of speech and of the press, the right of peaceable assembly, equality before the law...In them lies a spiritual right of men.

Behind them is the conception which is the highest development of the Christian faith - the conception of individual freedom with brotherhood.

President Franklin D. Roosevelt stated in his First Inaugural Address, March 4, 1933:

First of all, let me assert my firm belief that the only thing we have to fear is fear itself...In such a spirit on my part and on yours we face our common difficulties. They concern, thank God, only material things...Where there is no vision the people perish.(Pr. 29:18)...

We face arduous days that lie before us in the warm courage of national unity; with the clear consciousness of seeking old and precious moral values...In this dedication of a nation we humbly ask the blessing of God. May He protect each and every one of us! May He guide me in the days to come.

President Franklin D. Roosevelt told the Federal Council of Churches of Christ, December 6, 1933:

If I were asked to state the great objective which Church and State are both demanding for the sake of every man and woman and child in this country, I would say that that great objective is "a more abundant life."

In his Christmas Message, December 24, 1933, President Franklin D. Roosevelt stated:

This year marks a greater national understanding of the significance in our modern lives of the teachings of Him whose birth we celebrate. To more and more of us the words 'Thou shalt love thy neighbor as thyself' have taken on a meaning that is showing itself and proving itself in our purposes and daily lives.

May the practice of

that high ideal grow in us all in the year to come. I give you and send you one and all, old and young, a Merry Christmas and a truly Happy New Year. And so, for now and for always "God Bless Us Every One."

President Franklin D. Roosevelt stated on the 400th Anniversary of the Printing of the English Bible, October 6, 1935:

We cannot read the history of our rise and development as a Nation, without reckoning with the place the Bible has occupied in shaping the advances of the Republic. Its teaching, as has been wisely suggested, is ploughed into the very heart of the race.

Where we have been truest and most consistent in obeying its precepts we have attained the greatest measure of contentment and prosperity.

The Great Depression ended in the early 1940's, with the advent of World War II

28.
A BREAK IN THE CLOUDS AT THE PRECISE MOMENT LEADS TO VICTORY

President Franklin D. Roosevelt addressed Congress, December 8, 1941:

December 7, 1941 - a date which will live in infamy – the United States of America was suddenly and deliberately attacked by naval and air forces of the Empire of Japan...

The attack yesterday on the Hawaiian Islands has caused severe damage...lives have been lost...ships have been reported torpedoed between San Francisco and Honolulu...the Japanese government also launched an attack against Malaya...Hong Kong...Guam...Philippine Islands...Wake Island...and Midway Island...

Our people, our territory and our interests are in grave danger. With confidence in our armed forces, with the unbounding determination of our people, we will gain the inevitable triumph. So help us God.

FDR stated January 6, 1942:

Japan's...conquest goes back half a century...War against China in 1894...Occupation of Korea...War against Russia in 1904...Fortification of the mandated Pacific islands following 1920...Seizure of Manchuria in 1931...Invasion of China in 1937.

In his State of the Union, January 6, 1942, President Franklin D. Roosevelt stated:

Our enemies...know that victory for us means victory for the institution of democracy - the ideal of the family, the simple principles of common decency and humanity. They know that victory for us means victory for religion. And they could not tolerate that...

We must guard against complacency. We must not underrate the enemy. He is powerful and cunning - and cruel and ruthless. He will stop at nothing that gives him a chance to kill and to destroy...

We are fighting to cleanse the world of ancient evils...Our enemies are guided by brutal cynicism, by unholy contempt for the human race. We are inspired by a faith that goes back through all the years to the first chapter of the Book of Genesis: "God created man in His own image."

We on our side are striving to be true to that divine heritage. We are fighting, as our fathers have fought, to uphold the doctrine that all men are equal in the sight of God.

On January 25, 1941, President Franklin D. Roosevelt wrote the Prologue of a *Gideon's New Testament & Book of Pslams* that was distributed to millions of World War II soldiers:

To the Armed Forces: As Commander-in-Chief, I take pleasure in commending the reading of the Bible to all who serve in the armed forces of the United States. Throughout the centuries men of many faiths and diverse origins have found in the Sacred Book words of wisdom, counsel and inspiration. It is a fountain of strength and now, as always, an aid in attaining the highest aspirations of the human soul. Very sincerely yours, Franklin D. Roosevelt.

In 1942, Imperial Japan invaded Singapore and took 25,000 prisoners. Next was the Philippines. With Imperial Japan's relentless bombardment by planes and heavy siege guns, President Franklin D. Roosevelt did not want General Douglas MacArthur captured, so he ordered him to leave Corregidor, Philippines, and evacuate to Australia. General Douglas MacArthur obeyed, March 11, 1942, but not without promising, "I shall return."

The turning point in the Pacific War began June 4, 1942. American codebreakers intercepted intelligence of Imperial Japan's plans to capture Midway Island and from there, Hawaii and the rest of the Pacific. The outnumbered U.S. Pacific Fleet attempted a desperate ambush of the Imperial Japanese armada, but was losing badly.

When the Imperial Japanese fleet suddenly changed its course, the American torpedo dive-bombers searched for it in vain, with many of their escort fighters running out of fuel and ditching in the ocean.

Lieutenant-Commander John Waldron, who led the torpedo dive-bomber squadron from the U.S. carrier *Hornet,* told his men the night before:

> My greatest hope is that we encounter a favorable tactical situation, but if we don't, I want each of us to do our utmost to destroy the enemies. If there is only one plane to make a final run in, I want that man to go in and get a hit. May God be with us.

Waldron's squadron was the first to spot the Imperial Japanese fleet. Flying in at low altitude, they suffered the full force of Japanese defenses. Out of 30 of Waldron's men who took off that morning, only one survived. Waldron received the Navy Cross posthumously.

Their sacrifice was not in vain, as it benefited the other American torpedo dive-bomber squadrons from the U.S. carriers *Enterprise* and *Yorktown*, who arrived about an hour later, flying at a much higher altitude.

Navigating by guess and by God, and running low on fuel, squadron commander C. Wade McClusky, Jr., was determined to continue the search. Through a break in the clouds they providentially sighted far below a wake and followed it to find the Japanese aircraft carriers: *Akagi, Kaga, Soryu,* and *Hiryu.*

This was at the precise moment when most of the Imperial Japanese "Zero" fighter planes were busy being refueled and rearmed after fighting Waldron's squadron, or had just taken off to attack the U.S. carrier *Yorktown.*

In just five minutes, the screeching American torpedo dive-bombers sank three Imperial Japanese carriers, and a fourth shortly after. In just moments, Imperial Japan's naval force had been cut in half, resulting in their being forced to the defensive.

After the Battle of Midway, plans were begun to free the Philippines. During Imperial Japan's occupation of the Philippines, they forced Filipino and American prisoners on the horrible Bataan Death March, during which over 10,000 died.

When he heard of this, General Douglas MacArthur stated, April 9, 1942:

To the weeping mothers of its dead, I can only say that the sacrifice and halo of Jesus of Nazareth has descended upon their sons, and that God will take them unto Himself.

President Roosevelt said, August 12, 1943:

Three weeks after the armies of the Japanese launched their attack on Philippine soil, I sent a proclamation...to the people of the Philippines...that their freedom will be redeemed...The great day of your liberation will come, as surely as there is a God in Heaven.

On October 20, 1944, General Douglas MacArthur returned to the Philippines with U.S. troops, stating:

People of the Philippines: I have returned. By the grace of Almighty God our forces stand again on Philippine soil - soil consecrated in the blood of our two peoples. We have come, dedicated and committed to the task of destroying every vestige of enemy control...

The hour of your redemption is here...Let the indomitable spirit of Bataan and Corregidor lead on...Let no heart be faint. Let every arm be steeled. The guidance of Divine God points the way. Follow in His name to the Holy Grail of righteous victory!

President Roosevelt sent a message to Philippine President Osmena, October 20, 1944:

On this occasion of the return of General MacArthur to Philippine soil with our airmen, our soldiers, and our sailors, we renew our pledge. We and our Philippine brothers in arms - with the help of Almighty God - will drive out the invader; we will destroy his power to wage war again, and we will restore a world of dignity and freedom.

29.
WEATHER CLEARS AFTER
PATTON'S 250,000 TROOPS PRAY

President Franklin D. Roosevelt stated, December 21, 1941:

Looking into the days to come, I have set aside a Day of Prayer, and in that Proclamation I have said:

"The year 1941 has brought upon our Nation a war of aggression by powers dominated by arrogant rulers whose selfish purpose is to destroy free institutions. They would thereby take from the freedom-loving peoples of the earth the hard won liberties gained over many centuries.

"The new year of 1942 calls for the courage...Our strength, as the strength of all men everywhere, is of greater avail as God upholds us.

"Therefore, I...do hereby appoint the first day of the year 1942 as a day of prayer, of asking forgiveness for our shortcomings of the past, of consecration to the tasks of the present, of asking God's help in days to come.

"We need His guidance that this people may be humble in spirit but strong in the conviction of the right; steadfast to endure sacrifice, and brave to achieve a victory of liberty and peace."

In his State of the Union Address, January 6, 1942, President Roosevelt stated:

Our enemies are guided by brutal cynicism, by unholy contempt for the human race. We are inspired by a faith which goes back through all the years to the first chapter of the Book of Genesis - "God created man in His own image." We on our side are striving to be true to that Divine heritage.

We are fighting, as our fathers have fought, to uphold the doctrine that all men are equal in the sight of God. Those on the other side are striving to destroy this deep belief and to create a world in their own image, a world of tyranny and cruelty and serfdom.

Adolf Hitler had seized power in Germany in 1933 by promising hope after a depression and devaluation of their currency. His National Socialist Workers Party eliminated political opposition, took control of healthcare and confiscated guns. With lightning speed over two dozen countries were occupied. In 1,200 concentration camps over 4 million died.

The major turning point was D-Day, June 6, 1944, when 160,000 troops landed along a 50-mile stretch of heavily fortified Normandy coast. It was the largest invasion force in world history, involving 5,000 ships and 13,000 aircraft. The beaches of Omaha, Utah, Gold, Juno, Sword and Pointe du Hoc ran red with the blood of over 9,000 killed or wounded. Supreme Allied Commander Dwight Eisenhower ordered:

> You are about to embark upon the Great Crusade...The eyes of the world are upon you. The hopes and prayers of liberty-loving people everywhere march with you...You will bring about...the elimination of Nazi tyranny over the oppressed peoples of Europe...Your task will not be an easy one. Your enemy is well trained, well equipped and battle-hardened. He will fight savagely...And let us all beseech the blessings of Almighty God upon this great and noble undertaking.

President Franklin Roosevelt stated June 6, 1944:

My fellow Americans: Last night, when I spoke with you...I knew at that moment that troops of the United States and our allies were crossing the Channel in another and greater operation...I ask you to join with me in prayer: Almighty God, our sons, pride of our Nation, this day have set upon a mighty endeavor, a struggle to preserve our republic, our religion, and our civilization...Give strength to their arms, stoutness to their hearts, steadfastness in their faith. They will need Thy blessings. Their road will be long and hard. The enemy is strong. He may hurl back our forces...

We know that by Thy grace, and by the righteousness of our cause, our sons will triumph...Some will never return. Embrace these, Father, and receive them, Thy heroic servants, into Thy kingdom...

Help us, Almighty God, to rededicate ourselves in renewed faith in Thee in this hour of great sacrifice...

I ask that our people devote themselves in a continuance of prayer. As we rise to each new day, and again when each day is spent, let words of prayer be on our lips, invoking Thy help to our efforts. Give us strength...and, O Lord, give us Faith. Give us Faith in Thee...With Thy blessing, we shall prevail over the unholy forces of our enemy...And a

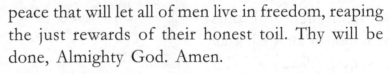

peace that will let all of men live in freedom, reaping the just rewards of their honest toil. Thy will be done, Almighty God. Amen.

A month after D-Day, an assassination of Hitler was attempted by courageous German resistance, but he survived and retaliated by executing over 7,000 Germans.

By December of 1944, Nazis amassed three armies for an enormous attack against the Allies in the Ardennes Forest and soon surrounded the 101 Airborne Division in southern Belgium, demanding their surrender. U.S. General Anthony McAuliffe answered in one word: "Nuts." This response confused the Nazi commander, causing him to hesitate.

Marching to the rescue was the U.S. Third Army,

but it was hindered due to bad weather. General Patton directed Chaplain James O'Neil to compose a prayer for his 250,000 troops to pray:

Almighty and most merciful Father, we humbly beseech Thee, of Thy great goodness, to restrain these immoderate rains... Hearken to us as soldiers who call upon Thee... Establish Thy justice among men and nations.

The weather cleared and the Allies were able to successfully counterattack. In his order, December 22, 1944, General Eisenhower stated:

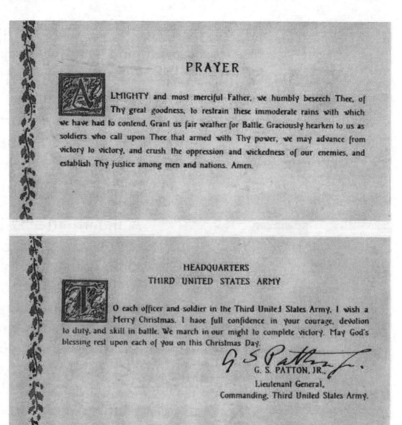

By rushing out from his fixed defenses the enemy may give us the chance to turn his great gamble into his worst defeat.

So I call upon every man, of all the Allies, to rise now to new heights of courage...with unshakable faith in the cause for which we fight, we will, with God's help, go forward to our greatest victory.

America's most decorated WWII combat soldier was 19-year-old Audie Murphy. Fighting in many battles, Audie saw his friend killed August 15, 1944, after which he grabbed a machine gun and stormed the enemy, wounding 2, killing 6, and taking 11 prisoners.

In September of 1944, he killed 4 and wounded 3 while taking an enemy machine gun position. In October of 1944, he captureed 2 before being shot in the hip by a sniper. Taking aim, he shot the sniper between the eyes.

Recovering, Audie single-handedly held off for over an hour an entire company of Nazi's at Colmar Pocket in France, January 14, 1945. Wounded again and out of ammunition, he led a counterattack.

Hitler's National Socialist Workers Party was finally defeated, May 8, 1945. Victory cost over 16 million Allied military deaths.

Audie Murphy wrote in his poem, "Alone and Far Removed":

> So long my comrades,
> Sleep ye where you fell upon the field.
> But tread softly please,
> March o'er my heart with ease,
> March on and on,
> But to God alone we kneel.

President Franklin Roosevelt had stated December 24, 1944:

> It is not easy to say 'Merry Christmas' to you, my fellow Americans, in this time of destructive war...We will celebrate this Christmas Day in our traditional American way...because the teachings of Christ are fundamental in our lives...the story of the coming of the immortal Prince of Peace.

30.
PRESIDENT TRUMAN THANKS GOD FOR WORLD WAR II VICTORY

President Truman declared a Day of Prayer, August 16, 1945:

> The warlords of Japan...have surrendered unconditionally... This is the end of the...schemes of dictators to enslave the peoples of the world... Our global victory...has come with the help of God... Let us...dedicate ourselves to follow in His ways.

General Douglas MacArthur, the Supreme Allied Commander in the Southwest Pacific, received Japan's surrender on the *USS Missouri* in Tokyo Harbor, September 2, 1945.

World War II left a death toll of over 70 million military and civilians on all sides. Lightning the National Christmas Tree, December 24, 1946, President Truman said:

> Our...hopes of future years turn to a little town in the hills of Judea where on a winter's night two thousand years ago the prophecy of Isaiah was fulfilled. Shepherds keeping watch by night over their flock heard the glad tidings of great joy from the angels of the Lord singing, "Glory to God in the Highest and on Earth, peace, good will toward men"...
>
> If we will accept it, the star of faith will guide us into the place of peace as it did the shepherds on that day of Christ's birth long ago...
>
> Through all the centuries, history has vindicated His teaching...In this great country of ours has been demonstrated the fundamental unity of Christianity and democracy.

In 1952, President Truman made the National Day of Prayer an annual event, stating:

> In times of national crisis when we are striving to strengthen the foundations of peace...we stand in special need of Divine support.

31.
FAITH DURING THE KOREAN WAR

"FREEDOM IS NOT FREE" is inscribed on the Korean War Memorial in Washington, D.C. The conflict began as a U.N. "police action," but soon escalated. The outnumbered U.S. and South Korean troops fought courageously against North Korean and Communist Chinese troops who were killing thousands with arms and MIG fighters supplied by the Soviet Union.

Five-star General Douglas MacArthur was Supreme U.N. Commander during the beginning of the Korean War. He made a daring landing of troops deep behind enemy lines at Inchon, then recaptured Seoul.

With temperatures sometimes forty degrees below zero, and Washington politicians limiting the use of air power against the Communists, there were nearly 140,000 American casualties in the defense of the Pusan Perimeter and Taego; in the landing at Inchon and the freeing of Seoul; in the capture of Pyongyang; in the Yalu River where nearly a million Communist Chinese soldiers invaded; in the Battles of Changjin Reservoir, Old Baldy, White Horse Mountain, Heartbreak Ridge, Pork Chop Hill, T-Bone Hill, and Siberia Hill.

Harry S Truman described communism in his Inaugural Address, January 20, 1949:

We believe that all men are created equal because they are created in the image of God. From this faith we will not be moved...

Communism is based on the belief that man is so weak and inadequate that he is unable to govern himself, and therefore requires the rule of strong masters.

Democracy is based on the conviction that man has the moral and intellectual capacity, as well as the inalienable right, to govern himself with reason and justice.

Communism subjects the individual to arrest without lawful cause, punishment without trial, and forced labor as a chattel of the state.

It decrees what information he shall receive, what art he shall produce, what leaders he shall follow, and what thoughts he shall think.

Democracy maintains that government is established for the benefit of the individual, and is charged with the responsibility of protecting the rights of the individual and his freedom...

These **differences between communism and democracy** do not concern the United States alone. People everywhere are coming to realize that what is involved is material well-being, human dignity, and the right to believe in and worship God.

On December 24, 1952, President Truman lit the National Christmas Tree, stating:

Tonight, our hearts turn first of all to our brave men and women in Korea. They are fighting and suffering and even dying that we may preserve the chance of peace in the world...Let us remember always to try to act and live in the spirit of the Prince of Peace. He bore no hate...nothing but love for all mankind. We should try as nearly as we can to follow His example.

We believe that all men are truly the children of God...

As we pray for our loved ones far from home - as we pray for our men and women in Korea, and all our service men and women wherever they are - let us also pray for our enemies. Let us pray that the spirit of God shall enter their lives and prevail in their lands...Through Jesus Christ the world will yet be a better and fairer place.

President Eisenhower's son, John Sheldon Doud Eisenhower, served in Korea during this time. First Lady Mamie Geneva Doud Eisenhower stated regarding their son:

He has a mission to fulfill and God will see to it that nothing will happen to him till he fulfills it.

The Korean War ended July 27, 1953, with the armistice signed at Panmunjom.

General Douglas MacArthur told West Point cadets, May 1962:

The soldier, above all other men, is required to practice the greatest act of

Korean War

religious training-sacrifice. In battle and in the face of danger and death, he discloses those Divine attributes which his Maker gave when He created man in His own image. No physical courage and no brute instinct can take the place of Divine help which alone can sustain him.

General MacArthur addressed the Salvation Army, December 12, 1951:

History fails to record a single precedent in which nations subject to moral decay have not passed into political and economic decline.

There has been either a spiritual awakening to overcome the moral lapse, or a progressive deterioration leading to ultimate national disaster.

32.
PRAYER DURING APOLLO MISSIONS

Apollo 8 Astronaut Frank Borman, during the first mission to fly around the moon, radioed back in December of 1968, looking back at the Earth from 250,000 miles away:

In the beginning, God created the heavens and the earth.

Apollo 11 blasted off from Cape Kennedy July 16, 1969, being the first mission to walk on the moon. In Proclamation 3919, President Richard Nixon stated:

Apollo 11 is on its way to the moon. It carries three brave astronauts; it also carries the hopes and prayers of hundreds of millions of people...That moment when man first sets foot on a body other than earth will stand through the centuries as one supreme in human experience...I call upon all of our people...to join in prayer for the successful conclusion of *Apollo 11*'s mission.

On July 20, 1969, Astronauts Neil Armstrong and Buzz Aldrin, landed their lunar module, the *Eagle*, and spent a total of 21 hours and 37 minutes on the moon's surface before redocking with the command ship *Columbia*. Neil Armstrong became the first man to walk on the moon, stating:

> One small step for a man, one giant leap for mankind.

Buzz Aldrin, in an interview with *Guideposts Magazine,* July 20, 1989, "A Meal on the Moon: A little-known fact about the Apollo Moon Landing," revealed that during the planned rest time in the *Eagle*, he had a private communion service:

> I silently read the Bible passage..."I am the Vine, you are the branches"...as I partook of the wafer and the wine, and offered a private prayer...I could think of no better way to acknowledge the enormity of the Apollo 11 experience than by giving thanks to God.

President Nixon spoke to the astronauts on the moon:

> This certainly has to be the most historic telephone call ever made from the White House...The heavens have become a part of man's world...For

one priceless moment in the whole history of man all the people on this earth are truly one...one in our prayers that you will return safely to Earth.

President Nixon greeted the astronauts on the *USS Hornet*, July 24, 1969:

The millions who are seeing us on television now...feel as I do, that...our prayers have been answered...I think it would be very appropriate if Chaplain Piirto, the Chaplain of this ship, were to offer a prayer of thanksgiving.

Addressing Congress, September 16, 1969, Commander Neil Armstrong stated:

To those of you who have advocated looking high we owe our sincere gratitude, for you have granted us the opportunity to see some of the grandest views of the Creator.

On April 11, 1970, *Apollo 13* was launched for the moon. Shortly thereafter came the message: "Houston, we've had a problem." Mission control identified that an oxygen tank had exploded, irreparably damaging the craft.

Special prayer services were held at the Chicago Board of Trade, at St. Peter's Basilica by the Pope, at the Wailing Wall in Jerusalem and reported in the *New York Times*. The U.S. Senate adopted a resolution urging prayer.

In April of 1970, President Richard Nixon had the nation observe a Day of Prayer for Apollo 13 astronauts.

In sub-zero temperature, the crew pieced together an oxygen filter, jump-charged the command module batteries, and manually steered the ship to land in the ocean near a raging hurricane.

On April 19, 1970, President Nixon spoke at Kawaiaha'o Church, one of the oldest Christian Churches in Hawaii:

> When we learned of the safe return of our astronauts, I asked that the Nation observe a National Day of Prayer and Thanksgiving today... This event reminded us that in these days of growing materialism, deep down there is still a great religious faith in this Nation...

I think more people prayed last week than perhaps have prayed in many years in this country...We pray for the assistance of God when... faced with... great potential tragedy.

On *Apollo 14*'s mission, February 1971, Astronaut Edgar Mitchell left a microfilm copy of the Bible on the moon's surface inside the lunar module *Antares*.

On *Apollo 16*'s mission, April 21, 1972, Astronauts Charles Duke and John Young explored the rugged Descartes region of the moon. Astronaut Charles Duke spoke at a Prayer Rally during the State's Republican Convention in San Antonio's Lila Cockrell Theatre, June 22, 1996:

I used to say I could live ten thousand years and never have an experience as thrilling as walking on the moon. But the excitement and satisfaction of that walk doesn't begin to compare with my walk with Jesus, a walk that lasts forever.

On October 28, 1998, at age 77, Astronaut John Glenn was aboard the Space Shuttle *Discovery,* becoming the oldest person to go into space. This was 36 years after he had become the first American to orbit the earth in 1962.

Observing the heavens and the earth from his window, John Glenn stated:

> To look out at this kind of creation and not believe in God is to me impossible. It just strengthens my faith.

In 2010, NASA was working on the *Constellation* program, building new rockets and spaceships capable of returning astronauts to the moon. President Obama cancelled it. On June 30, 2010, Administrator Charles Bolden outlined the new priorities for NASA in an interview with the Middle East News agency in Cairo, *Al Jazeera:*

> When I became the NASA administrator...President Obama charged me...perhaps foremost...to find a way to reach out to the Muslim world and engage much more with dominantly Muslim nations to help them feel good.

Though manned space exploration may be on hold, we cannot forget the tremendous scientific achievements and courage those who dared to go into the unknown, and the prayers of faith that bore them up.

———◆———

CONCLUSION
PRAYER FOR MIRACLES IN AMERICA
TODAY AND BELIEVE GOD WILL ANSWER

At a time when the highest office is discontinuing the tradition of a National Day of Prayer event at the White House, yet celebrating Islamic Ramadan, reducing the military, discounting nuclear threats, disregarding rights of conscience, promoting policies resulting in job loss and economic decline, filling positions affecting national security with individuals having questionable connections to the Muslim Brotherhood, appointing socialist-leaning czars, and increasing national debt to unprecedented levels, all must pray to save the nation.

The Bible chapters of Deuteronomy 28 and Leviticus 26 list the blessings on a nation which hearkens to the voice of the Lord, and the judgments for not.

Second Chronicles 7:14 states: "If my people, which are called by my name, shall humble themselves, and pray, and seek my face, and turn from their wicked ways; then will I hear from heaven, and will forgive their sin, and will heal their land."

Try to lead everyone you know to a real relationship with God the Father through His son Jesus while there is still time. THE ONLY THING YOU CAN TAKE TO HEAVEN ARE THE SOULS YOU LEAD TO JESUS.

Please pray the prayer below and add your own prayers as you are led by the Holy Spirit:

Our Dear Heavenly Father, in Jesus' Name we come humbly before You and ask Your forgiveness for our sins and the sins of our nation. We acknowledge that You are Lord of lords, King of kings, the One True God. We ask that you touch the hearts of our leaders to turn to You and do Your will. We ask that they come to know Jesus as their personal Lord and Savior and seek to follow Your Word. We ask that You give us a President who will serve You, uphold Your commandments and love and protect Your people. Help us to love our enemies.

We pray for the Senate, Congress, Judges and all elected and unelected officials at the Federal, State, county and city levels. May they hear Your voice and give You their lives in service to America, one nation under God. May they not follow their own political ambitions but serve out of love for their fellow man. Lord, help us to replace the leaders who have only selfish ambitions with God-fearing servants who respect life at all stages. Satan, we bind you in Jesus' Name from influencing our leaders.

Dear Lord, protect our country, especially our borders, from terrorists and those who plot evil. We ask that You give charge to Your angels to protect us from all harm, in Jesus' Name. Defend Israel and we pray for the peace of Jerusalem.

Jesus, we thank You for dying and shedding Your blood to cleanse us of our sins and deliver us from the evil one - Satan. We cover this entire country with the blood of Jesus to shield us from evil.

Jesus, thank You for rising so that we may have eternal life. Thank you for our daily bread.

Lord, strengthen us and our families to be the heroes of America today. May we be witnesses of Your love, grace, strength and power.

Thank You Father. We love You. Thy will be done. In Jesus' mighty Name we pray. Amen.